Intelligent Inclusion

Designing accessible

future with AI

Deepali Bhavale

BlueRose ONE.com
Stories Matter
NewDelhi • London

BLUEROSE PUBLISHERS
India | U.K.

For permissions requests or inquiries regarding this publication, please contact:

BLUEROSE PUBLISHERS
www.BlueRoseONE.com
info@bluerosepublishers.com
+91 8882 898 898
+4407342408967

ISBN: 978-93-7018-731-3

Cover Design: Aman Sharma
Typesetting: Pooja Sharma

First Edition: May 2025

Author's Note

This book isn't just about AI or accessibility – it's about people. It's about the incredible lives that have shaped mine and inspired every word on these pages.

To my amazing **parents** – thank you for being the first ones to show me what true inclusion looks like. Your lifelong dedication to supporting the disabled community has been my greatest teacher. Everything I know about empathy, courage, and service comes from watching you lead with heart.

To my brothers –

Rahul Bhaiya, you have been so much more than a brother to me. You've been my role model, my protector, and a quiet force of wisdom in my life. I am endlessly grateful for the impact you've had on my life.I carry your strength with me wherever I go.

Rohan, thank you for being my roots and my wings. You've always been there, cheering me on quietly but fiercely.

To **Amol**, my partner in every sense – thank you for being my calm, my sounding board. Your faith in me never wavered, even when mine did. This book wouldn't exist without your constant encouragement.

To **Aditi** – your curiosity, kindness, unconditional love and fearless spirit reminds me every day of the future we're building.

And to **Simba** – my furry love, your companionship and unconditional love has brought warmth and joy through our lives.

This book is for all of you – and for everyone who dares to imagine a more inclusive world.

With love and gratitude,

Deepali

Preface / Introduction

Intelligent Inclusion: Designing Accessible Futures with AI

> "*The true power of technology is not in what it can do, but in who it empowers.*"

In a world increasingly shaped by intelligent systems, the promise of **Artificial Intelligence** (AI) extends far beyond convenience or automation — it reaches into the heart of **human dignity, equality, and access**. As we build machines that learn, adapt, and make decisions, a critical question emerges: *Are we building for everyone?*

Accessibility — the principle of designing systems that everyone, regardless of ability or disability, can use — has too often been an afterthought. Yet, with AI's transformative potential, we have a once-in-a-generation opportunity to change that. To move from retrofitting inclusion to **intelligent inclusion** — weaving accessibility into the fabric of innovation itself.

This book is a **call to action** for developers, designers, educators, researchers, policymakers, and dreamers. It explores the evolving intersection of AI and accessibility — not just as a technical challenge, but as a **moral and societal imperative**.

We'll journey through:

- The fundamentals of AI and how they apply to **visual, auditory, motor, and cognitive accessibility**

- Real-world examples and **case studies** of AI empowering individuals with disabilities
- Hands-on projects that show how to **build accessible AI systems**
- The ethical complexities, biases, and design principles involved in creating technology that truly includes

Whether you are building a sign language recognition app, designing a voice assistant that understands more voices, or simply curious about how AI can create a better world — this book is your companion and guide.

Together, let's shift the narrative from accessibility as accommodation to **accessibility as innovation** — and build a future that works for **everyone**.

Contents

Chapter 1: What is Accessibility?

1.1 Understanding Accessibility

In its simplest form, **Accessibility** refers to the design and provision of a service, product, or environment that is usable by people regardless of their abilities or limitations. This includes people with disabilities, but also encompasses a broader range of individuals, such as those with sensory, cognitive, or physical impairments, as well as those with temporary limitations. Essentially, accessibility aims to ensure that everyone can access and engage with something, whether it's a website, a building, or a product, with equal ease and effectiveness.

For many, accessibility is often mistaken for just "adding captions to videos" or "supporting screen readers." While those are important, true accessibility goes much deeper. It is a philosophy, a **design mindset**, and a **responsibility** – not just a checklist item.

Accessibility asks:

- Can a blind user interact with your app using a screen reader?
- Can a deaf user access the information in your video?
- Can a person with dyslexia read your website without getting overwhelmed?
- Can someone with limited mobility navigate your product with only keyboard input?

In short, accessibility is about **removing barriers** and **empowering independence**.

True accessibility is proactive. It means planning for users with various needs from the **initial design phase** instead of retrofitting accessibility features as afterthoughts. It acknowledges that disability is not an exception, but a natural part of human diversity.

Accessibility is also **intersectional**. A user might be dealing with multiple conditions simultaneously, like being blind and having limited mobility, or being neurodiverse while also dealing with anxiety. Designing with flexibility in mind improves usability for **everyone** – including people using mobile devices in bright light, aging users with diminishing abilities, or someone using your product in a noisy environment.

1.2 Categories of Disabilities (with Examples)

To design accessible technologies, we must first understand the types of challenges people may face:

Category	**Examples**
Visual	Blindness, low vision, color blindness
Auditory	Deafness, hard of hearing
Motor/Physical	Limited mobility,tremors,paralysis

Cognitive	Dyslexia, ADHD, memory loss, autism
Speech	Stuttering, muteness, voice disorders

Each of these categories may affect how someone uses a computer, app, or AI-powered system. For example:

- A person with blindness may rely on screen readers, which need semantic HTML and accessible labels.
- A person with cognitive impairments may need simplified language and distraction-free interfaces.
- Someone with a motor disability may use voice commands or alternative input devices like sip-and-puff switches.

Moreover, some disabilities are **temporary or situational**. A broken arm, a loud train ride, or bright sunlight on a screen – all introduce accessibility needs. Designing inclusively helps everyone.

Categories of Disabilities

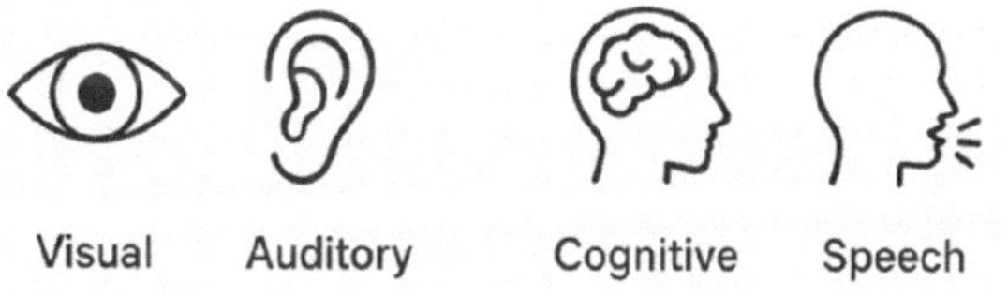

1.3 Why Accessibility Matters

- **1 in 6 people** worldwide experience a significant disability (WHO)
- The global disability community includes over **1.3 billion people**
- Inclusive design increases **user satisfaction for everyone**, not just people with disabilities
- Accessibility leads to **better SEO, performance, and user retention**
- In many countries, it's not just ethical – it's the **law** (e.g., ADA, WCAG, RPWD Act in India)

Accessibility isn't just a moral obligation – it's a business imperative. Inclusive products reach wider markets, improve customer loyalty, and help companies stand out. Studies show that accessible design often enhances usability across the board, increasing conversions and reducing abandonment rates.

Beyond metrics, it's also about **human dignity**. The web and software should be **equalizers**, not gatekeepers. When we build with empathy, we enable more people to learn, work, communicate, and live with autonomy.

> *"Accessibility is not just a feature. It's a fundamental right."*

1.4 Accessibility in India and Developing Countries

While accessibility is a global concern, it takes on even greater significance in countries like **India** and other developing nations, where:

- The **digital divide** is still wide

- Infrastructure is unevenly distributed
- Awareness and enforcement of accessibility standards are limited
- Disabilities are often stigmatized or underreported

According to the **2011 Indian Census**, over **2.2% of India's population** lives with a disability – though many experts believe the actual number is much higher due to underreporting. With the rise of **Digital India** and increasing internet penetration, it's crucial that we ensure **inclusive access** to digital resources, services, education, healthcare, and opportunities.

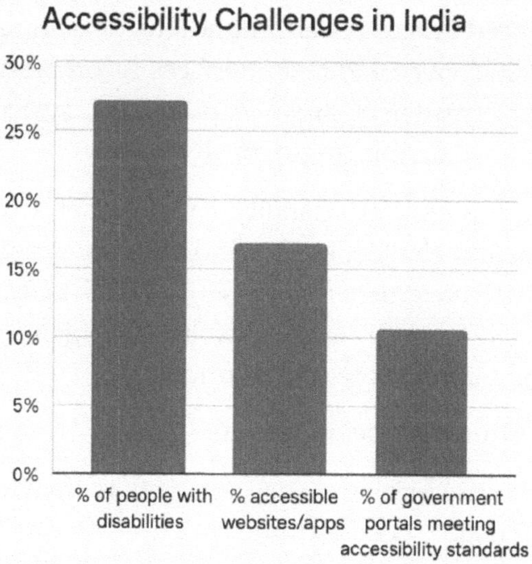

Figure: Accessibility Challenges in India

Common Challenges in India:

- Lack of awareness among developers and designers
- Low priority given to accessibility in project lifecycles
- Limited availability of assistive technologies in rural areas
- Accessibility not integrated into **UI/UX or product design workflows**
- Inconsistent support for Indian languages in assistive tools (like screen readers)

Accessibility in India also faces linguistic challenges. With 22 official languages and hundreds of dialects, building accessible voice and text interfaces is complex. Tools like screen readers and captioning systems must accommodate this **linguistic diversity**.

In rural areas, affordability and internet access further compound challenges. A blind child in a remote village may not have access to basic assistive tools. Here, AI-powered mobile apps can become **game changers**, offering offline, low-cost solutions.

1.5 Cultural & Social Barriers

Beyond technical issues, accessibility is often hindered by **cultural and social attitudes**:

- Disabilities are sometimes viewed as taboos or misfortunes
- Many individuals with disabilities **hide their challenges**, fearing discrimination

- Families and communities may discourage independence
- Schools and workplaces may not provide accommodations

This makes the role of **inclusive technology even more powerful**. AI can offer personalized, stigma-free, low-cost solutions – from sign language detection to text-to-speech in regional languages.

> *"Where society erects barriers, technology can build bridges."*

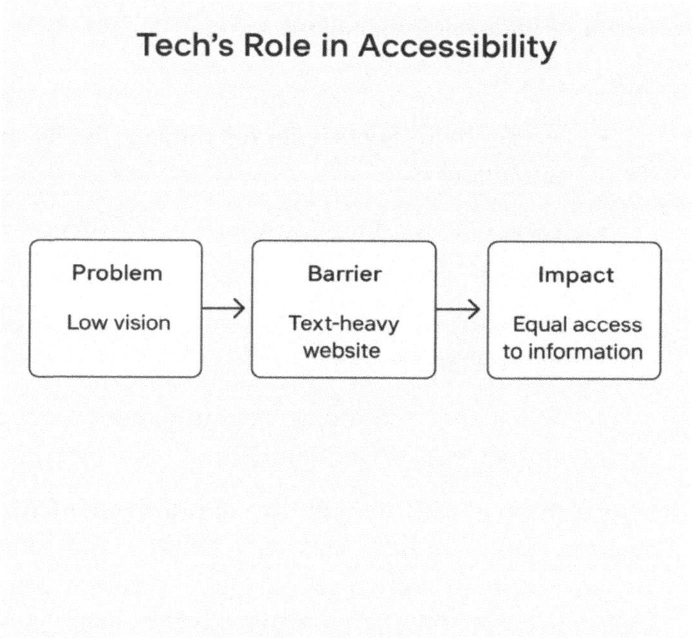

Figure: Tech's Role in Accessibility

To drive change, we must address the **ecosystem** – including education systems, policy makers, product developers, and the community at large. Accessibility should not only be a feature but a **standard expectation** in every product, from public portals to e-commerce platforms.

Chapter Summary

This chapter laid the foundation for understanding what accessibility means, especially in a digital and AI-powered world. We explored its definitions, categories, global importance, and how it plays out uniquely in the Indian context. We also examined cultural, social, and infrastructural challenges that shape the accessibility narrative in developing nations.

Key takeaways:

- Accessibility is essential for human dignity and autonomy
- Designing for disability improves experiences for everyone
- The barriers are not just technical – they're also cultural and systemic
- India and developing countries need tailored, inclusive AI-driven solutions

As we move ahead, we will dive into the **role of AI in making accessibility smarter, faster, and more personalized** – ultimately shaping a future where inclusion is not optional, but embedded into every line of code and design decision.

Chapter 2: The Role of AI in Accessibility

2.1 Introduction to Assistive Technologies

Assistive technologies have long served as critical tools for individuals with disabilities, enabling them to interact with their environments more independently and effectively. Traditional aids such as screen readers, Braille keyboards, and hearing aids marked important advancements, yet many of these solutions remained limited in adaptability, personalization, and scalability.

With the emergence of artificial intelligence (AI), assistive technologies are undergoing a transformative shift. AI brings to the table capabilities such as contextual understanding, real-time adaptation, and

predictive analysis, allowing for a more intuitive and inclusive experience. This chapter explores how AI technologies are revolutionizing accessibility, with examples that illustrate both the power and promise of intelligent inclusion.

2.2 Traditional vs. AI-Powered Assistive Technologies

Traditional Assistive Technologies

- **Static functionality:** Limited to pre-programmed tasks
- **High cost and limited distribution:** Often expensive and inaccessible in developing regions
- **Minimal personalization:** Devices and software offered uniform experiences regardless of the user's unique needs

AI-Powered Assistive Technologies

- **Adaptive intelligence:** Learn from user behavior and environment
- **Greater scalability and affordability:** Leveraging mobile and cloud technologies
- **Highly personalized experiences:** Customizes solutions for individual needs, improving engagement and effectiveness

2.3 Key AI Technologies Enabling Accessibility

Natural Language Processing (NLP)

NLP enables voice-controlled systems, real-time transcription, and language translation. Applications include:

- Voice assistants for visually impaired users
- Real-time captioning tools for the deaf and hard of hearing

Computer Vision (CV)

CV helps interpret and describe the world visually. Examples include:

- Object recognition systems to help blind users navigate spaces
- Sign language recognition for bridging communication gaps

Speech Recognition and Synthesis

These technologies convert speech to text and vice versa, supporting:

- Voice-driven interfaces
- Reading assistants for those with dyslexia or cognitive impairments

Machine Learning (ML)

ML enables systems to improve over time by learning from data, empowering:

- Personalized learning platforms
- Predictive accessibility features, such as gesture-based controls

2.4 Case Studies and Applications

Case Study 1: Seeing AI by Microsoft

Overview:

Seeing AI is an AI-powered mobile application developed by Microsoft that serves as a digital guide for people with visual impairments. The app narrates the world around the user by recognizing and describing people, objects, scenes, and even text in real-time using computer vision.

Technical Insight:

- **Core Technologies:** Computer Vision, Optical Character Recognition (OCR), Facial Recognition
- **Key AI Features:** Real-time object detection, scene interpretation, currency recognition, handwriting reading

Real-World Impact:

Ravi, a blind university student from India, uses Seeing AI to independently navigate his college campus. The app describes the location of entrances, identifies professors by name using facial recognition, and reads out notices on bulletin boards. For Ravi, it replaces the need for constant human assistance and gives him newfound independence.

Challenges and Successes:

- **Challenges:** Difficulty recognizing objects in low-light or cluttered environments
- **Successes:** High accuracy in document scanning and facial recognition makes it widely adopted globally

Case Study 2: Google Live Transcribe

Overview:

Live Transcribe is an Android application by Google that provides real-time speech-to-text transcription to assist people who are deaf or hard of hearing. It captures spoken words through the device microphone and transcribes them instantly on screen.

Technical Insight:

- **Core Technologies:** Automatic Speech Recognition (ASR), Natural Language Processing
- **Key AI Features:** Multilingual support (over 80 languages), ambient sound detection (e.g., doorbell, fire alarm)

Real-World Impact:

Megha, a hard-of-hearing high school teacher, uses Live Transcribe to communicate with hearing students. During lectures, the app captures students' questions and displays them in real-time, allowing her to respond without lip-reading or interpretation services. The app has become her go-to communication tool in professional and social settings.

Challenges and Successes:

- **Challenges:** Inaccuracies in noisy environments or with overlapping conversations
- **Successes:** Enhanced inclusivity in classrooms and meetings across many cultures and languages

Case Study 3: Avaz – An Indian AAC App for Speech Disabilities

Overview:

Avaz is a picture-based Augmentative and Alternative Communication (AAC) app developed in India, primarily used by children with autism, cerebral palsy, and other developmental conditions. It enables non-verbal users to construct sentences using images and predictive text.

Technical Insight:

- **Core Technologies:** Predictive modeling, Natural Language Processing, UX personalization
- **Key AI Features:** Learning user behavior, suggesting next words or images based on context

Real-World Impact:

Ananya, a 7-year-old non-verbal child in Chennai, struggled to express basic needs and emotions. With

Avaz, she can now construct complete sentences like "I want to play outside" or "I feel sad." Her parents note improved emotional stability and reduced frustration since she began using the app.

Challenges and Successes:

- **Challenges:** Initial setup and training require parental involvement and educator support
- **Successes:** Has been translated into multiple Indian languages and used in over 40 countries

2.5 Visuals and Diagrams

Comparative Table – Traditional vs. AI-Powered Assistive Technology

Aspect	Traditional Assistive Technologies	AI-Powered Assistive Technologies
Core Technology	Rule-based systems, hardware-driven aids	Machine learning, deep learning, NLP, computer vision
Adaptability	Static; limited to predefined inputs	Highly adaptive; learns and improves with use
Personalization	One-size-fits-all approach	Tailored to individual user needs and behavior
Language Support	Often limited to dominant languages	Supports multiple regional and sign

		languages using NLP
Real-Time Capability	Delayed or manual interaction required	Real-time translation, prediction, and interaction
Cost	Can be expensive due to custom hardware	Cost-effective with scalable software solutions
Maintenance	Requires physical servicing	Remote updates and self-improving systems
Use Cases	Screen readers, hearing aids, Braille displays	Sign language detection, voice-to-text apps, intelligent tutoring systems
User Learning Curve	Often steep due to rigid interfaces	Intuitive, voice/gesture/natural interaction-enabled
Scalability	Difficult to scale geographically and linguistically	Easily scalable across regions and languages with cloud/edge AI

Inclusivity Potential	Basic support, limited scope	Holistic inclusion through contextual and cultural understanding

How AI Enhances Accessibility

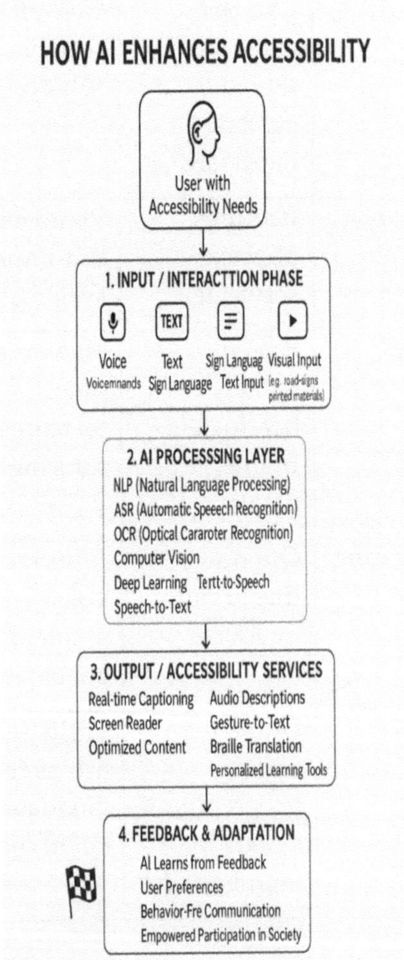

Categories of AI Applications in Accessibility

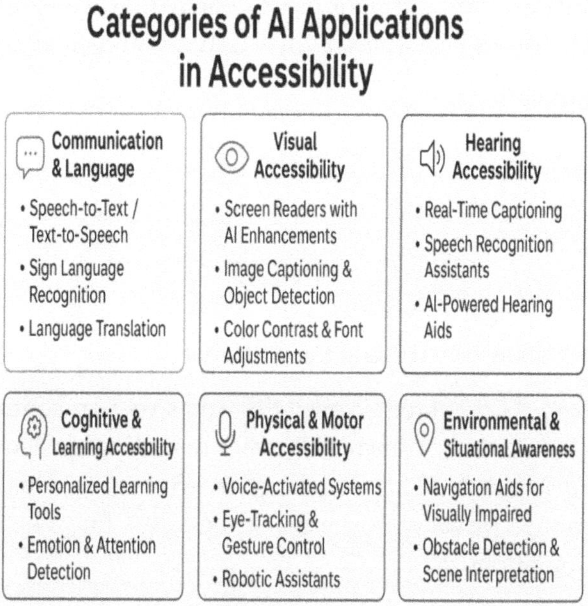

2.6 Risks, Biases, and Ethical Considerations

While the integration of AI into accessibility technologies offers tremendous benefits, it also raises significant ethical and social concerns. It is imperative to evaluate and address these risks to ensure that technological advancements do not inadvertently exacerbate inequality.

2.6.1 Algorithmic Bias

AI systems are only as good as the data they are trained on. If the training data contains biases — whether related to gender, race, language, or disability — the resulting models may reinforce or even amplify those biases. For instance, a speech recognition system trained predominantly on voices from a particular demographic may perform poorly for users outside that group, such as individuals with speech impairments or accents.

Implications:

- Unequal access to services
- Lower user trust and engagement
- Marginalization of underrepresented communities

2.6.2 Data Privacy and Surveillance

Many AI-powered accessibility tools rely on continuous data collection – including voice recordings, video feeds, and location data – to function effectively. This raises serious privacy concerns, especially for vulnerable populations.

Ethical Questions:

- Who owns the data?
- How is it stored and protected?
- Can it be used to surveil users without consent?

2.6.3 Over-Reliance on Technology

AI can complement human support but cannot replace the empathy, understanding, and contextual awareness that human caregivers and educators provide. Over-reliance on technology could lead to:

- Reduced social interaction
- Dependency on systems that may not always work

- Loss of traditional support networks

2.6.4 Accessibility of AI Tools Themselves

Ironically, many AI tools are not accessible to the very users they aim to support. Poor UI/UX design, lack of multilingual support, and non-inclusive content formats can hinder adoption and usability.

Recommendations:

- Involve persons with disabilities in design and testing
- Adhere to WCAG and universal design principles
- Provide alternative interaction modes (voice, touch, visual)

2.6.5 Ethical Frameworks and Governance

To responsibly develop and deploy AI for accessibility, organizations must adopt ethical frameworks that prioritize fairness, accountability, transparency, and inclusiveness.

Key Initiatives:

- Explainable AI (XAI): Ensure users understand how decisions are made
- AI ethics committees and review boards
- Policies for inclusive AI development and audits

2.7 Future Outlook and Trends

The future of AI in accessibility is not just promising—it is transformative. As technology evolves, we are poised to witness unprecedented levels of inclusion across education, employment, healthcare, and daily life.

Emerging trends indicate a shift from assistive to **inclusive technologies**, where accessibility becomes a default feature rather than a retrofit.

2.7.1 Multimodal AI for Seamless Interaction

Future accessibility tools will increasingly leverage **multimodal AI**, combining vision, audio, text, and haptics to offer richer, more context-aware user experiences. For example:

- **Smart wearables** that translate sign language into speech in real-time using computer vision and motion sensors.
- **Ambient AI systems** that interpret surroundings and deliver alerts through visual, auditory, or tactile feedback based on user preference.

2.7.2 Hyper-Personalization and Context Awareness

Advancements in **context-aware computing** and real-time behavioral analysis will allow AI systems to adapt dynamically to individual needs. This includes:

- Predicting user intent and offering proactive assistance (e.g., auto-suggesting navigation routes based on past behavior).
- Learning emotional and cognitive states through voice, gesture, or facial analysis to provide empathetic responses.

2.7.3 AI-Driven Universal Design

There is a growing movement towards embedding AI into the principles of **Universal Design**—products and services that are accessible to all, without the need for adaptation. Examples include:

- Automatically adjusting reading interfaces based on visual acuity and reading patterns.
- AI-curated educational content tailored to different learning disabilities and cognitive profiles.

2.7.4 Decentralized and Edge AI Solutions

To address concerns around privacy, latency, and connectivity, **Edge AI**—AI computation done locally on devices—is becoming a game changer. Benefits include:

- Real-time accessibility services in low-connectivity regions
- Greater control over personal data, crucial for populations with higher vulnerability

2.7.5 Inclusive AI Research and Co-Creation

The future of AI in accessibility must be shaped **with** people with disabilities, not just **for** them. Co-creation models are emerging where:

- Users actively participate in the development, testing, and refinement of AI tools.
- Open-source accessibility datasets and community-driven innovation play a central role in inclusive research.

2.7.6 Policy and Ethical Foresight

As AI capabilities expand, there will be increasing emphasis on regulatory frameworks that:

- Mandate accessibility standards in AI product design
- Encourage inclusive procurement and funding practices
- Foster international collaboration to ensure equitable access to AI-powered assistive technologies across geographies

Chapter 3: Designing Accessible AI Systems

3.1 Introduction

As artificial intelligence becomes increasingly embedded in the fabric of daily life, ensuring that these systems are accessible from the ground up is not merely beneficial—it is essential. Accessibility cannot be an afterthought. Designing AI for accessibility requires an intentional, inclusive, and multi-dimensional approach that spans user research, technical architecture, interface design, testing, and policy integration. This chapter explores the core principles, challenges, and best practices for designing AI systems that truly serve everyone, especially persons with disabilities.

3.2 Principles of Inclusive Design

Inclusive design goes beyond simply accommodating disability—it is about creating systems that anticipate and embrace human diversity. The following principles guide the development of accessible AI systems:

1. Equitable Use

Ensure the design is useful and marketable to people with diverse abilities.

2. Flexibility in Use

Provide choice in methods of use, including voice, gesture, text, and touch interfaces.

3. Simple and Intuitive Use

Eliminate unnecessary complexity in user interfaces and language.

4. Perceptible Information

Design for clarity using multiple modes (text, visuals, audio, haptics) to convey information.

5. Tolerance for Error

Minimize hazards and unintended actions; allow users to undo or correct errors easily.

6. Low Physical Effort

Reduce unnecessary physical interaction or reliance on fine motor skills.

7. Size and Space for Approach and Use

Ensure reach, manipulation, and comfort regardless of the user's mobility or environment.

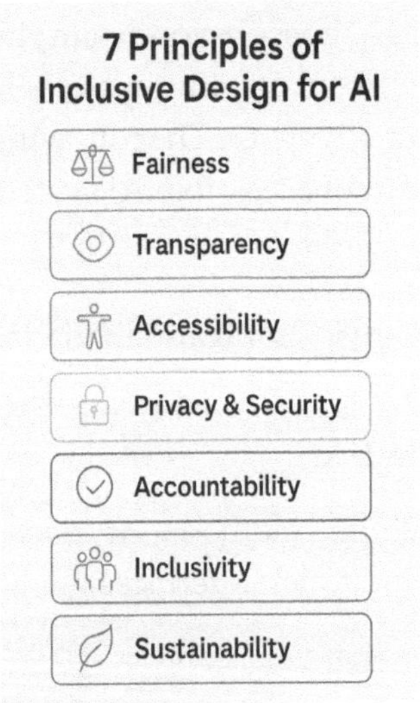

"7 Principles of Inclusive Design for AI"

3.3 Co-Creation with People with Disabilities

One of the most effective ways to build inclusive systems is to co-create them with the intended users. Co-creation is a participatory process where users with disabilities are involved throughout the product lifecycle—from ideation and prototyping to deployment and evaluation.

Benefits of Co-Creation:

- Identifies real pain points
- Prevents bias and assumptions
- Builds empathy within development teams
- Improves product adoption and satisfaction

Best Practices:

- Partner with disability organizations and schools
- Use accessible prototyping tools
- Employ participatory design sessions and usability testing
- Compensate users for their contributions

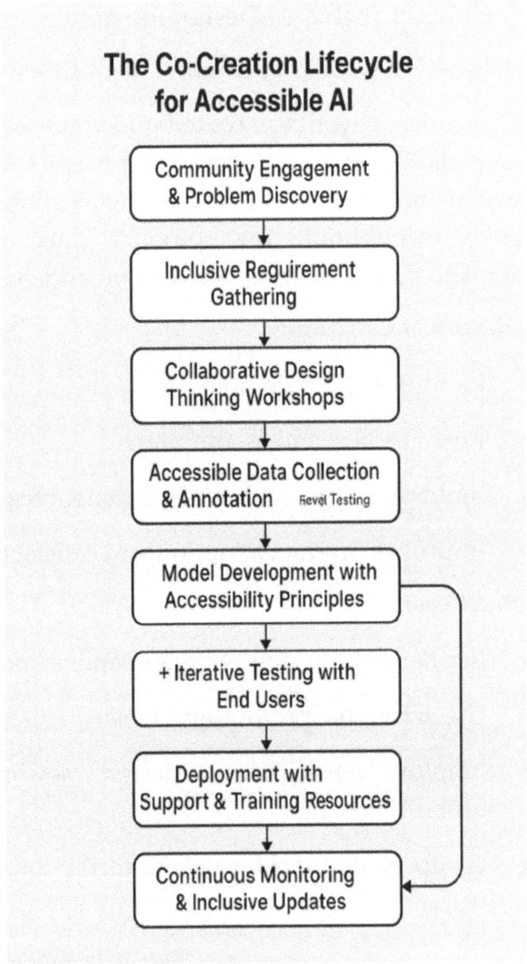

3.4 Designing Multimodal Interfaces

Multimodal interfaces combine multiple input and output methods—such as speech, text, visuals, and haptics—to cater to different user needs and preferences. Designing AI systems with multimodal interaction greatly enhances usability and accessibility.

Key Modalities:

- **Voice**: Speech recognition and synthesis
- **Text**: Transcripts, captions, and chat interfaces
- **Visuals**: Icons, images, color-coded indicators
- **Haptics**: Vibration alerts, tactile feedback

Guidelines:

- Allow switching or combining modes based on user preference
- Avoid over-reliance on a single mode (e.g., visuals only)
- Ensure consistency and synchronization between modes

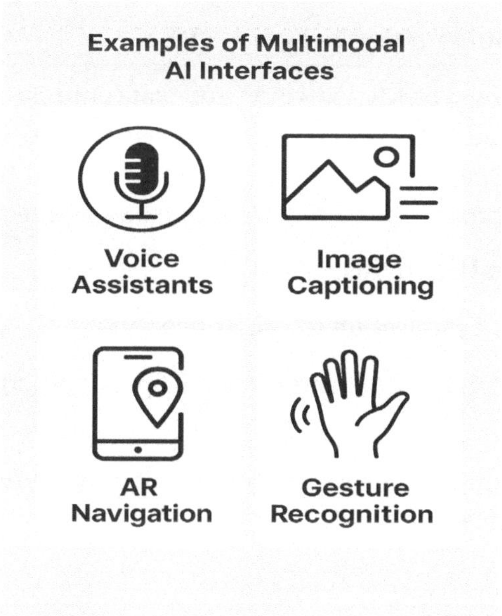

3.5 Case Studies in Accessible AI Design

Case Study 1: SignAble – ISL Interpretation App

Overview: SignAble is an Indian mobile application providing real-time Indian Sign Language interpretation for video calls. It connects users with certified ISL interpreters, enabling more accessible communication.

Design Highlights:

- Minimal UI for ease of use
- Multilingual support
- On-demand human interpreter integration

Impact: Deaf individuals can now participate in job interviews, medical consultations, and family conversations with greater independence.

Case Study 2: Be My Eyes + GPT-4

Overview: Be My Eyes is an app that connects blind users with sighted volunteers for assistance. The integration with OpenAI's GPT-4 Vision allows for real-time visual description without requiring human volunteers.

Design Highlights:

- Seamless image interpretation
- Contextual and natural language responses

Impact: Significantly reduces dependency on availability of volunteers, providing immediate and private visual assistance.

Case Study 3: Alexa for Accessibility (Amazon)

Overview: Amazon has expanded Alexa's voice recognition to better serve users with speech impairments and regional accents.

Design Highlights:

- Personalized voice training
- Voice profile creation
- Localized content

Impact: Improved experience for users with non-standard speech patterns or multilingual households.

Case Study 4: Eye-Controlled Navigation by Microsoft

Overview: Eye Control, built into Windows, allows users to navigate the interface using only their eyes, enabled through eye-tracking hardware.

Design Highlights:

- Dwell-based clicks
- On-screen keyboard
- Predictive text support

Impact: People with mobility impairments (e.g., ALS patients) can now use computers for communication and work more independently.

3.6 Testing for Accessibility in AI

Accessibility testing ensures that AI systems are usable by people with a wide range of disabilities. This goes beyond WCAG compliance and includes interaction patterns, data model fairness, and response accuracy.

Testing Approaches:

- **Automated Tools**: Use AI-powered tools like Microsoft Accessibility Insights, axe-core, and WAVE
- **Manual Audits**: Conduct keyboard-only navigation tests, screen reader evaluations, and visual clarity assessments
- **User Testing**: Involve users with disabilities in real-world scenarios
- **AI Fairness Audits**: Evaluate model bias for different user groups

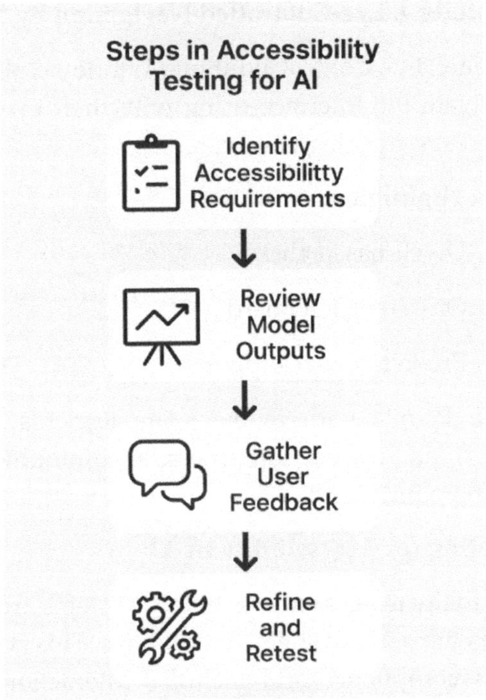

3.7 Integration into Development Lifecycle

Designing accessible AI is not a one-off task. It must be embedded into every stage of the development lifecycle:

1. Requirements Gathering

- Include accessibility goals and user stories
- Identify user personas with disabilities

2. Design and Prototyping

- Use inclusive patterns
- Simulate disabilities (e.g., colorblind filters, screen readers)

3. Development

- Implement semantic HTML, ARIA roles, keyboard navigation
- Use labeled datasets inclusive of diverse users

4. Testing and Validation

- Run accessibility and bias tests alongside functionality testing

5. Deployment and Monitoring

- Provide accessible onboarding materials
- Collect feedback and iterate

6. Governance and Accountability

- Assign accessibility champions
- Track metrics like accessibility score, issue resolution rate

Chapter 4: The Architecture of AI Assistive Technologies

4.1 Introduction

Artificial Intelligence has not only improved the accuracy of assistive technologies—it has redefined what is possible. From screen readers that adapt to user behavior, to wearable devices that guide individuals through urban environments, AI enables systems that are increasingly intelligent, adaptive, and personalized. This chapter dives into the architecture and engineering behind these tools, evaluating the categories, techniques, and infrastructure considerations that power AI-driven accessibility.

4.2 Categories of AI Assistive Technologies

AI-driven assistive technologies can be grouped based on the primary human function they augment or compensate for:

1. Visual Assistance

- Object and scene recognition (e.g., using CNNs)
- Text-to-speech (OCR + NLP)
- Navigation support with spatial mapping

2. Auditory Assistance

- Real-time speech-to-text captioning
- Voice amplification and filtering
- Sound classification alerts (e.g., doorbells, alarms)

3. Mobility and Motor Support

- Eye-tracking or brain-computer interface navigation
- AI-powered prosthetics and exoskeletons
- Path planning using reinforcement learning

4. Cognitive and Learning Assistance

- AI tutors with personalized learning pathways
- Emotion recognition to adjust difficulty or pace
- Predictive task reminders and automated scheduling

4.3 AI Techniques Behind Assistive Tools

Different types of AI power various aspects of these tools:

- Convolutional Neural Networks (CNNs): For image classification, object detection, facial recognition (used in visual tools).
- Recurrent Neural Networks (RNNs) & Transformers: For speech recognition, language modeling, and predictive typing.
- Natural Language Processing (NLP): Enables comprehension, summarization, translation, and voice command interpretation.
- Reinforcement Learning: Personalized interactions by adapting behavior based on rewards and feedback loops.
- Multimodal Fusion Models: Combine input types (e.g., video + audio) to create richer, context-aware systems.

4.4 Integrating AI Tools into Real-World Infrastructure

AI assistive technologies are most impactful when embedded in the fabric of daily environments:

Smart Classrooms

- AI captioning and translation tools (real-time speech-to-text, multilingual output)
- Gesture recognition to support students with mobility impairments

Healthcare Settings

- Diagnostic support for visually impaired healthcare workers
- NLP-based interfaces for non-verbal patients

Public Infrastructure

- Smart kiosks with voice-guided navigation
- AI-driven apps for real-time transit assistance
- Visual signage readers for the blind

4.5 Comparative Analysis: AI vs Traditional Assistive Tech

Feature	Traditional Assistive Tech	AI-Powered Tools
Adaptability	Static	Learns and adapts to user behavior
Real-Time Response	Often delayed	Instantaneous or near real-time

Multilingual Support	Limited	Broad multilingual support
Cost	Often lower	Higher, but falling with scale
Personalization	Minimal	High (predictive, adaptive systems)

4.6 Limitations and Ethical Concerns

Despite their promise, AI assistive technologies bring their own challenges:

Bias and Fairness

AI systems trained on non-diverse datasets may misinterpret or exclude disabled users.

Privacy and Surveillance

Continuous data capture (especially vision/audio) raises concerns over user consent and misuse.

Over-Dependence

Users may become reliant on AI systems that are prone to failure or require constant updates.

Accessibility of the Assistive Tools

Ironically, some tools require modern smartphones, fast internet, or high literacy—putting them out of reach for many.

4.7 Future of AI-Driven Assistive Technology

Looking ahead, the next wave of assistive technologies promises even greater integration and inclusivity:

Multilingual and Multi-Disability Tools

AI systems will increasingly support multiple disabilities simultaneously, with robust multilingual functionality.

On-Device AI and Edge Computing

Reduced latency and offline functionality through embedded AI chips (e.g., in hearing aids or smart glasses).

Emotionally Intelligent AI

Systems that understand user frustration, fatigue, or mood to adjust support dynamically.

Robotic Companions

AI-integrated robotic devices that support emotional well-being, physical assistance, and task automation.

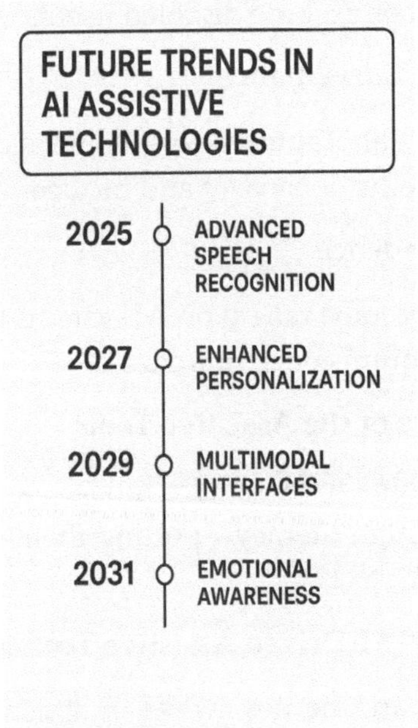

Chapter 5: Evaluating Accessibility in AI Systems

5.1 Introduction

As artificial intelligence becomes deeply embedded in our everyday tools, its role in enabling—or obstructing—accessibility grows ever more significant. Simply building AI-driven tools isn't enough; they must be evaluated through a rigorous, inclusive lens. This chapter explores the key methodologies, challenges, and strategies involved in assessing the accessibility of AI systems, especially those built for or impacting people with disabilities.

5.2 Universal Design Principles in AI Contexts

Universal design is the foundation for accessibility. Applying it in AI contexts means creating systems that are usable by the widest range of people possible, without needing adaptations or specialized design.

Core Principles Applied to AI:

1. Equitable Use:

   AI systems should not privilege one group over another. For example, an AI voice assistant must understand diverse accents and dialects equally well.

2. Flexibility in Use:

   AI interfaces should adapt to user preferences—e.g., providing multiple interaction modes (voice, touch, gesture) for users with different abilities.

3. Simple and Intuitive Use:

   AI systems must avoid overwhelming complexity. For example, screen reader outputs should be optimized for clarity and brevity.

4. Perceptible Information:

   Visual outputs should be accompanied by auditory alternatives, and vice versa.

5. Tolerance for Error:

   AI should allow for mistake recovery—e.g., predictive text tools that learn from user corrections without rigid penalties.

6. Low Physical Effort:

   AI-based applications must reduce the amount of effort required to interact—important for users with mobility impairments.

7. Size and Space for Approach and Use:

   Interfaces, both digital and physical (like AI kiosks), should consider reach and space for wheelchair users or those with visual limitations.

5.4 Automated Accessibility Testing Tools

With the rise of AI, accessibility evaluation itself can be partially automated. These tools not only speed up testing but offer scalability and standardization.

Key AI-enabled tools and their features:

- Axe-core & Axe DevTools (Deque Systems):

  Offers browser extensions for automated WCAG rule checks on web apps. AI is used to detect patterns missed by hard-coded rules.

- Microsoft Accessibility Insights:

  Uses AI to scan desktop and web applications for common accessibility failures and provides detailed remediation guidance.

- Google's Lighthouse + AI Plugins:

  AI-enhanced Lighthouse plugins perform audits that detect low-contrast text, missing alt attributes, and navigation traps.

- AI-Powered Image Analysis Tools:

  These tools generate alt text automatically by using computer vision to describe images. (E.g., Facebook's automatic alt text system.)

- Voice Accessibility Testing:

  Simulated voice assistant interactions test for speech clarity, natural language understanding, and fallback strategies when inputs fail.

Limitations:

- They don't replace human judgment.
- Context-sensitive issues are still best assessed manually.
- Cannot assess cognitive load or emotional accessibility effectively yet.

5.5 Human-Centered Evaluation Frameworks

AI accessibility must be validated through real user experiences. Human-centered evaluation frameworks go beyond compliance—they measure usability, comfort, and emotional response.

Popular Frameworks:

- User Experience Questionnaire (UEQ):

  Evaluates accessibility in terms of attractiveness, efficiency, dependability, and stimulation.

- System Usability Scale (SUS):

  Widely used, especially in low-resource settings to evaluate effectiveness of AI interfaces.

- Inclusive AI Assessment Toolkit (Beta by MIT):

  Combines quantitative and qualitative data from diverse users to measure accessibility, interpretability, and fairness.

- Heuristic Evaluation for AI UIs:

  Uses experts to evaluate systems against a tailored set of accessibility heuristics specific to AI-based interaction.

Real-World Practice: User testing with assistive tech users—blind testers, deaf users with interpreters, or elderly users—is crucial. Feedback loops must be embedded in development cycles.

5.7 Real-World Accessibility Metrics for AI

When deploying AI systems, the following metrics help determine real-world accessibility impact:

1. Error Rate by Disability Type:

   Measuring how often the AI fails for different groups (e.g., speech misinterpretation rates for deaf users vs. hearing users).

2. Time-to-Task Completion:

   A measure of how long it takes users with disabilities to complete actions vs. abled users.

3. Perceived Effort and Satisfaction:

   Collected via post-task surveys, reflecting how accessible the user felt the system was.

4. Fallback Success Rate:

   AI should offer alternative methods when one modality fails (e.g., voice fails, but keyboard navigation succeeds).

5. Cognitive Load Analysis:

   Evaluates mental effort required using eye tracking, number of interactions, or subjective reporting.

6. Assistive Tech Compatibility Score:

   A composite metric measuring how well AI systems function across different screen readers, magnifiers, Braille displays, etc.

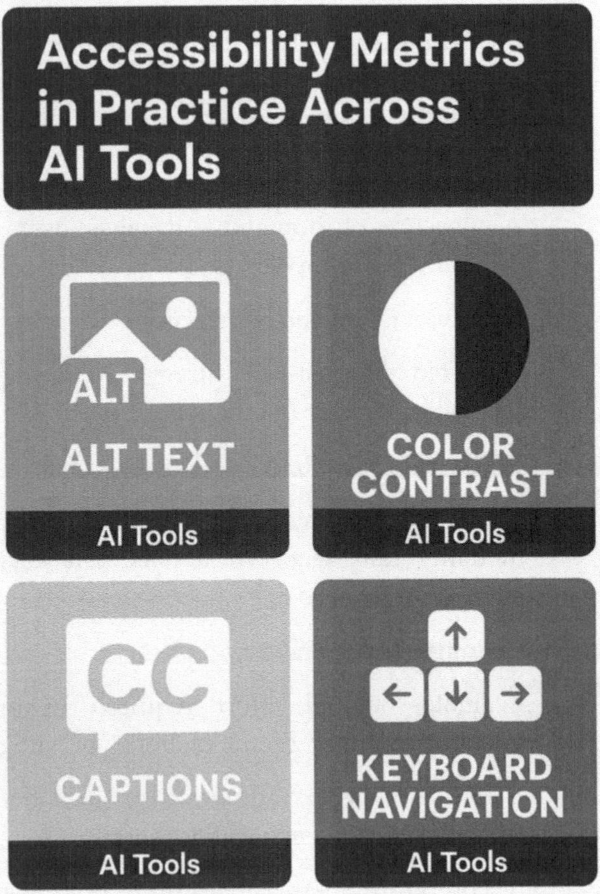

5.8 Cultural and Linguistic Considerations

Accessibility isn't just about ability—it's also about language, context, and local norms.

Why it matters:

- Multilingual AI Systems:

  AI must support not just translation, but interpretation of culturally specific context, idioms, or emotion.

- Voice Interface Bias:

  Many speech-to-text models struggle with regional accents or tonal languages. This creates a barrier for rural or tribal populations.

- Cultural Perceptions of Disability:

  In some cultures, disability is highly stigmatized, and users may hesitate to disclose needs—AI systems must be designed with anonymity and sensitivity.

- Design Localization:

  Accessibility interfaces must align with local color perceptions (e.g., red for danger, or red for celebration), content layout (left-to-right vs right-to-left), and text size norms.

5.9 Feedback-Driven Design: The Continuous Loop

Building truly accessible AI requires systems to learn *with* users, not just *for* them.

Feedback Mechanisms in AI Accessibility:

- Real-Time Feedback Collection:

  In-app satisfaction surveys, problem flags, or emotional sentiment analysis after interaction.

- Adaptive Learning:

  AI interfaces should learn from behavior and modify layout, prompts, or response styles. E.g., longer wait times for cognitive disabilities.

- Community Co-Design Workshops:

  Regular engagement with diverse users, including disabled communities, to test and iterate on features.

- Ethical Reporting Channels:

  Channels to report exclusion, bias, or inaccessibility must be transparent and accessible.

Chapter 6: Designing for Multi-Disability Use Cases

6.1 Introduction

Accessibility isn't one-size-fits-all—and the reality is that many individuals live with multiple disabilities simultaneously. A person might be both deaf and visually impaired, or have limited mobility coupled with a cognitive disorder. While AI has made great strides in addressing singular disability experiences, designing for overlapping or intersecting disabilities remains one of the most challenging yet critical frontiers.

This chapter explores the principles, patterns, and practices for building AI solutions that serve people with multiple, layered access needs. We move beyond siloed assistive features and towards holistic, flexible, and adaptive AI systems that can dynamically accommodate a spectrum of user experiences.

6.2 Understanding Multi-Disability Intersections

What constitutes "multi-disability"?

Multi-disability refers to any combination of:

- Sensory impairments (e.g., vision + hearing)
- Motor and cognitive impairments
- Communication and behavioral conditions
- Temporary + permanent + situational impairments

These combinations may amplify access barriers or require competing accommodations, making universal design especially crucial.

Real-world examples:

- A deaf-blind user navigating a mobile app
- A wheelchair user with dyslexia attempting to complete a form
- A neurodivergent person with mobility issues needing calm, minimal interfaces

6.3 Challenges in Designing for Multi-Disability Scenarios

1. Conflicting Modalities

- Voice commands aren't helpful for users who are non-verbal.
- Visual UI adaptations may not benefit blind users, and vice versa.

2. Context Switching

Users with cognitive disabilities may find it overwhelming to switch between different UI modes or devices for each need.

3. Lack of Representation in Datasets

Multi-disability scenarios are rarely captured in AI training datasets, resulting in biased or incomplete models.

4. Assistive Technology Overlap

Users may already be using several assistive devices or apps—integrating seamlessly with these tools is non-trivial.

6.4 Principles for Inclusive Multi-Disability Design

a. Flexibility in Input & Output

Allow multiple input and output modes—e.g., gesture + keyboard + speech + touch + haptic feedback.

b. Personalization by Default

Systems should learn and adapt to the user's preferences over time—automatically switching to the most appropriate mode.

c. Layered Accessibility

Provide layered accessibility features so users can combine what works for them:

- Captioning + Sign Language Avatars
- Haptic alerts + screen magnification
- Audio description + easy-read summaries

d. Consistent and Predictable Interactions

Consistency helps reduce the learning curve for users who rely on muscle memory or cognitive routines.

6.5 AI Approaches to Multi-Disability Design

1. Multimodal AI

Systems that can understand and generate multiple types of data (audio, video, text, gestures) are ideal for handling diverse user inputs/outputs.

Example: An AI assistant that recognizes facial expressions, understands typed input, and provides spoken or tactile responses.

2. Context-Aware Personalization

Using contextual signals like time of day, device being used, or recent interactions to dynamically adapt interfaces.

Example: At night, a visual-first interface automatically switches to a haptic-first or voice-first one for visually impaired users.

3. Adaptive UI Engines

AI-driven UI systems that rearrange layout, size, color contrast, and navigational complexity based on user needs in real-time.

6.6 Case Studies

🔍 Case Study 1: Microsoft Seeing AI – A Multimodal AI Powerhouse

Background

Microsoft's *Seeing AI* is a free mobile app that uses the device's camera and AI to narrate the world for people who are blind or have low vision. However, its real strength lies in supporting users with intersecting disabilities—for example, individuals who are blind and have cognitive or motor impairments.

Accessibility Features for Multi-Disability Users

1. Multimodal Interaction

- Input: Camera + voice commands + touchscreen

- Output: Speech + vibration feedback + large text
- This multimodal design supports users who may prefer or require one channel over another—or use a combination. For example, a user with low vision and mild speech impairment can still interact using text + camera input.

2. Modular Scene Understanding

- Seeing AI splits tasks into modules ("Short Text", "Product", "Person", "Scene", etc.), minimizing cognitive overload by allowing task-focused UI. This is especially useful for users with cognitive disabilities or memory issues.

3. Haptic Alerts

- Subtle vibrations confirm image capture and object detection, making it usable even for deaf-blind users with partial sensory input.

4. Low-Literacy Friendly

- The app uses icon-based UI and audio feedback to reduce dependence on reading skills—important for users with dyslexia or intellectual disabilities.

Technical Details

- Built on Microsoft's Azure Cognitive Services (OCR, Face API, Object Recognition).
- Edge-device optimizations for offline use—critical for those without continuous internet access.

- Uses AI model switching for different modules based on use-case.

Impact

- Widely adopted by blind communities, but also used by stroke survivors, individuals with autism, and older adults with cognitive + visual decline.
- A clear example of a multi-functional tool, not tied to a single diagnosis.

🔍 Case Study 2: Waymap - AI-Powered Indoor Navigation for Deaf-Blind Users

Background

Waymap is a navigation platform originally built for blind users but has evolved into a tool that redefines independence for individuals who are both deaf and blind—a group that faces significant mobility and communication barriers.

Key Accessibility Innovations

1. No GPS Needed

- Waymap uses sensor fusion (accelerometers, gyroscopes, barometers, and magnetometers) in smartphones to deliver turn-by-turn directions with <1 meter accuracy—both indoors and outdoors.

This is crucial because GPS doesn't work well in enclosed spaces like malls or transit stations, where deaf-blind individuals are most vulnerable.

2. Haptic and Tactile Navigation

- Directions are delivered via vibration patterns that communicate:
  - Left/Right turns
  - Obstacles ahead
  - Approaching destination
- The haptic language is customizable and trainable per user—supporting those with different tactile sensitivity or cognitive understanding levels.

3. No Reliance on Audio or Visuals

- Unlike other navigation tools (Google Maps), Waymap is designed to work without screens or audio, making it ideal for:
  - Completely blind + deaf users
  - Low-literacy or elderly users with sensory degradation

Technical Stack

- AI + inertial navigation + SLAM (Simultaneous Localization and Mapping)
- Open APIs to integrate with municipal transit and public infrastructure
- Accessible via smartphones or future wearable formats

Outcomes

- Piloted in cities like London, Washington D.C., and Vienna.

- Reported to increase independent travel frequency by over 60% among participants with dual sensory impairments.

🔍 Case Study 3: Google Action Blocks – Cognitive + Motor Accessibility in a Touch

Background

Google Action Blocks is a lesser-known but powerful accessibility feature in Android that allows users to create custom home screen buttons to perform complex actions (e.g., call mom, play music, get directions).

Originally designed for users with cognitive disabilities, it has become a cornerstone tool for those with combined motor and cognitive impairments.

How It Works

- Users (or caregivers) set up a block tied to a Google Assistant command.
- Each block is represented by an image or symbol on the home screen.
- A single tap triggers the whole sequence, replacing complex multi-step tasks.

Accessibility Features for Multi-Disability Users

1. Custom Visual Symbols

- Users with cognitive conditions like autism, Alzheimer's, or Down syndrome often struggle with language. Action Blocks allows adding photos or emojis as symbols, reducing the cognitive demand.

2. One-Tap Interaction

- This is a game changer for users with fine motor skill challenges (e.g., cerebral palsy, Parkinson's), as they don't need to navigate nested menus or type.

3. Routine Building and Predictability

- Helps build daily routines via scheduled blocks. Supports users who struggle with executive function, memory, or emotional regulation.

4. Caregiver Integration

- Caregivers can remotely manage the blocks, ensuring usability while preserving independence.

Technical Insights

- Powered by Google Assistant API and Android Accessibility Suite
- Integrates with TalkBack and other assistive tech
- Offline-capable for critical functions (e.g., emergency calls)

Impact

- Used in special education, elder care, and mental health recovery programs.
- Praised for offering high agency with low cognitive/motor demand, a rare combination in the tech ecosystem.

6.7 Strategies for Teams Designing Multi-Disability Solutions

- Build cross-disability personas during product design.
- Conduct co-design sessions with real users experiencing multiple disabilities.
- Employ modular accessibility layers that can be toggled or stacked.
- Perform scenario-based testing with combinations of impairments rather than single-axis assessments.

6.8 Open Challenges and Design Gaps in Multi-Disability AI Tools

While AI holds enormous potential for accessibility, it still falls short in critical areas—especially for users with multiple, overlapping disabilities. These users are often underrepresented in both design and testing.

⚠ 1. Dataset Diversity and Representation

Most training datasets do not include:

- Speech data from users with slurred or stuttered speech.
- Gestures from users with limited mobility.
- Screen interaction patterns from people with visual *and* cognitive impairments.

Implication: AI systems struggle with recognition and prediction when tested with such diverse inputs.

"If your dataset doesn't include me, your product doesn't support me."

— Feedback from a user with cerebral palsy and visual impairment.

🧩 2. Lack of Interdisciplinary Collaboration

Building effective tools for multi-disability users requires:

- Speech therapists, occupational therapists, and neuropsychologists
- Working alongside data scientists, UX designers, and AI engineers

Gap: These disciplines often operate in silos, leading to products that are either technically sound but inaccessible, or clinically relevant but poorly implemented.

🧠 3. Inadequate AI Explainability

For users with cognitive disabilities, transparency in how decisions are made is essential.

Challenges:

- Most models function as "black boxes."
- Users may not understand why the AI made a suggestion, refused a command, or failed to respond.

Needed:

- Explainable AI (XAI) tailored to cognitive levels.
- Visual + auditory representations of AI reasoning.

🌐 4. Connectivity Dependence

Many AI tools require:

- Stable internet
- Cloud-based inference
- Frequent updates

This excludes users in low-income or rural areas, or those who rely on assistive tech in disconnected environments.

🛠 5. Customization Barriers

AI systems rarely allow:

- Per-user tuning of interaction pace, interface layout, or assistive preferences.

Users with overlapping disabilities often need granular control—but interfaces don't support it (especially on mobile platforms).

🧪 6. Lack of Real-World Testing

Tools are often tested in labs or limited user trials.

Reality: Multi-disability users interact in noisy, complex, unpredictable environments—homes, schools, public spaces.

What's needed:

- Longitudinal testing
- In-situ feedback collection
- Continuous iteration with real users

6.9 Conclusion

Designing AI for multi-disability use cases is the ultimate test of empathy, creativity, and engineering discipline. It demands more than compliance—it calls for co-creation, context-awareness, and continuous learning. In embracing the complexity of human diversity, we not only build for those most marginalized but also enhance usability for all.

Chapter 7: Policy, Standards, and Ethical Frameworks for Accessible AI

7.1 Introduction

AI-driven accessibility is not just a technical challenge—it's a regulatory and ethical imperative. As AI becomes embedded into everything from government services to healthcare, ensuring it is accessible to *everyone*, including people with disabilities, is a legal requirement, a moral obligation, and a strategic advantage.

This chapter explores global and regional standards, governance structures, and ethical frameworks that shape how accessible AI is defined, regulated, and implemented.

7.2 Key Global Accessibility Standards

◆ 1. Web Content Accessibility Guidelines (WCAG)

Developed by the W3C, WCAG sets the benchmark for digital accessibility:

- Perceivable: Information must be presented in ways users can perceive (e.g., alt text, captions).
- Operable: Interface must be usable via keyboard, switch controls, or voice.
- Understandable: Language and navigation must be predictable and clear.
- Robust: Must work across platforms and with assistive technologies.

Though WCAG is not AI-specific, it underpins most digital inclusion efforts and is increasingly referenced in AI UX design.

◈ **2. ISO 9241 & ISO/IEC 40500**

- ISO 9241: Human-centered design processes for interactive systems.
- ISO/IEC 40500: International standard equivalent of WCAG 2.0.

These standards guide hardware/software design and interaction protocols for inclusivity in AI systems.

◈ **3. Americans with Disabilities Act (ADA), Section 508 (US)**

- ADA: Requires equal access to digital systems, which now includes AI-driven interfaces in government and education.
- Section 508: Federal agencies must ensure electronic and information technology is accessible to people with disabilities.

◈ **4. Rights of Persons with Disabilities Act (India)**

Mandates non-discrimination and equal opportunity in ICT systems, including apps and websites powered by AI. Accessibility audits are increasingly being applied to AI-based digital platforms under this act.

7.3 AI-Specific Ethical Frameworks

While most accessibility standards predate the AI era, several newer frameworks directly address AI ethics and intersect with disability inclusion:

⊛ UNESCO's AI Ethics Framework

Calls for:

- Inclusivity in training data
- Avoidance of algorithmic bias
- Transparency and explainability in decision-making

It explicitly mentions people with disabilities as a vulnerable group needing targeted protection.

⊛ European Union AI Act (Upcoming)

- Proposes a risk-based classification of AI systems.
- Requires high-risk systems (e.g., education, healthcare) to undergo accessibility evaluations.
- Emphasizes human oversight and access to redress mechanisms for marginalized groups.

7.4 Institutional Roles in Accessibility Governance

◆ Government Regulators

- Enforce standards (e.g., India's DEPwD, US Dept. of Justice)
- Fund inclusive innovation (e.g., AI4Accessibility challenges)

◈ Academia & Standards Bodies

- Develop methodologies for evaluating AI fairness and accessibility
- Create benchmark datasets inclusive of disabilities

◈ **Civil Society & NGOs**

- Conduct independent audits and accessibility evaluations
- Provide feedback loops via user testing panels

7.5 Auditing and Compliance in Accessible AI

📌 The Current State of AI Audits

AI auditing is a rapidly growing field, but accessibility often remains on the sidelines. Traditional AI audits focus on:

- Bias & Fairness: Ensuring the model doesn't discriminate by race, gender, or geography.
- Explainability: Making sure models can justify their decisions.
- Data Provenance: Verifying how and where data was collected.

However, accessibility rarely appears as a core audit metric. This is problematic because a system can be fair, explainable, and high-performing—yet still completely unusable for a person with a disability.

🔍 What Should an Accessibility Audit for AI Include?

A robust AI accessibility audit must go beyond compliance checklists:

1. Multi-Disability Usability Testing

- Test across visual, auditory, cognitive, and motor disabilities.

- Include assistive technologies like screen readers, braille displays, eye-trackers, and speech interfaces.

2. Algorithmic Accessibility Bias Analysis

- Does the model underperform for speech impaired users?
- Are image classifiers poor at recognizing gestures used by people with disabilities?
- Does NLP struggle with atypical sentence constructions (e.g., from neurodivergent users)?

3. Inclusive Data Provenance

- Does training data include sufficient samples from disabled individuals?
- Were data annotations done in collaboration with accessibility experts?

4. Adaptive UI Audit

- Are interfaces responsive to assistive input methods?
- Does the system degrade gracefully when accessibility tools are activated?

5. Real-World Context Simulation

- Does the tool perform well in noisy environments for deaf users?
- Can vision-based tools handle low-light or non-standard settings?

⚠ **Challenges**

- Lack of Tools: No standard tooling exists to simulate diverse disabilities during testing.
- Invisibility of Failures: Failures of accessibility are often not captured in accuracy metrics.
- Cost and Complexity: Comprehensive accessibility audits are seen as expensive and time-consuming.

7.6 Rights-Based Design and Disability Justice

⊛ From Compliance to Co-Creation

A truly inclusive AI system must go beyond "compliance." It must center the lived experiences of people with disabilities from day one.

This means following the principles of disability justice, a movement that emerged to challenge the limitations of both mainstream disability rights and conventional design.

🔍 Core Tenets of Rights-Based AI Design

1. Nothing About Us Without Us

- Disabled users must not just test the tool, but co-lead its design and development.
- Include disability advocates and domain experts on product teams and ethics panels.

2. Affirming Intersectionality

- A blind woman in a rural area faces different barriers than a blind urban male.

- Tools must acknowledge compound marginalizations (disability + race + gender + location).

3. Agency and Autonomy

- AI tools must enable choice, not replace it.
- Features like autoplay, forced speech input, or automated correction can disempower users if not implemented with consent.

4. Data Sovereignty

- People with disabilities should own and control their data.
- Implement mechanisms for data access, deletion, and portability, especially when biometric data (e.g., gesture, voice, eye movements) is used.

💡 Real-World Example

A startup developing an AI sign language interpreter included deaf community leaders in data collection, trained on Indian Sign Language, and allowed users to control how their gestures were stored. This co-design approach yielded higher engagement and adoption.

7.7 Emerging Trends in Policy and Regulation

Governments, corporations, and global institutions are beginning to recognize the urgency of accessible AI regulation.

☑ Trends to Watch

◈ 1. Mandatory AI Accessibility Statements

- Similar to environmental disclosures, companies may soon be legally required to disclose how accessible their AI systems are.

◈ 2. Accessibility-First Procurement Policies

- Public sector contracts now often require WCAG or ISO compliance.
- Example: Indian Railways mandates accessible ticketing platforms—even if they use AI chatbots or dynamic pricing engines.

◈ 3. Accessibility Sandboxes

- These are experimental zones (like the UK's "AI Accessibility Sandbox") where developers can:
    - Test AI products with live panels of disabled users
    - Get real-time feedback
    - Obtain precertification before launch

◈ 4. Third-Party Accessibility Auditors

- A growing market of certification bodies is emerging to offer:
    - Accessibility scoring for AI tools
    - Assistive tech compatibility reports
    - Compliance tracking dashboards

◆ 5. Litigation and Class Actions

- As awareness grows, legal pressure is rising:
  - Lawsuits over inaccessible websites and AI tools (e.g., job platforms not usable via keyboard)
  - Increased demand for accessible AI under consumer protection laws

7.8 Future Directions and Recommendations

The future of accessible AI hinges on a multi-layered strategy combining technology, policy, education, and accountability.

🚀 Strategic Recommendations

✅ 1. Global Accessibility Certification for AI

- A universal label like "Accessible AI Certified", similar to Energy Star or FDA approval.
- Could be managed by an international body (e.g., UN, ISO).

✅ 2. Accessibility as a Metric in Model Evaluation

- Include metrics like gesture recognition accuracy for limb-different users, voice input tolerance, and screen reader compatibility in standard ML benchmarks.

✅ 3. Accessibility Dataset Repositories

- Create global, open-access, multilingual datasets that:

- Include diverse accents, signs, gestures, and communication styles
- Are annotated with community oversight

☑ **4. Fund Interdisciplinary AI & Disability Research**

- Support centers that combine:
  - Computer Science
  - Disability Studies
  - Design Thinking
  - Policy and Law

☑ **5. Legally Mandated AIA (Accessibility Impact Assessments)**

- Every AI system in critical domains (health, education, transport) should be required to undergo a formal AIA, similar to environmental or data impact assessments.

Chapter 8: Designing AI for the Margins

8.1 Introduction

AI has been marketed as a universal solution—but in practice, it's often built for the average user, using average data, and designed by teams with limited exposure to the fringes of society. Those "at the margins"—disabled individuals, linguistic minorities, rural populations, neurodivergent users—are rarely included in the development lifecycle. This leads to tools that exclude the very people they could benefit most.

This chapter explores a transformative approach to AI design: one that *starts* from the margins. Rather than adapting mainstream systems to serve underserved communities, it proposes designing from the edge inward—prioritizing people with the most complex needs first. The result is often better for everyone.

8.2 Who Are 'the Margins' in AI?

People systematically underserved by current AI systems:

- People with disabilities (especially those with multiple or invisible disabilities)
- Speakers of low-resource languages
- Rural and low-connectivity populations
- Elderly users unfamiliar with digital systems
- Neurodivergent and non-verbal users

- Women and LGBTQ+ individuals in biased datasets
- Low-literacy and non-literate users

Margins ≠ Small Numbers

For example, India has:

- Over 20 crore people with disabilities
- 1,600+ languages, most unsupported in NLP tools
- Millions of users who interact with digital tools non-visually or non-textually

Designing for these groups is not just ethical—it's also scalable, global, and economically impactful.

8.3 Why AI Fails at the Margins

📉 1. Data Imbalance

- Training data is urban, English-centric, male-dominated, and sighted/hearing-abled.
- Signs of poor data: misclassification of sign language, misrecognition of regional accents, hallucinated speech transcription for dysarthric voices.

🤖 2. Lack of Model Adaptability

- Many AI systems are brittle; they cannot adapt to unexpected input styles (like gestures or eye movements).
- Low personalization for atypical user behaviors.

3. Design Team Homogeneity

- Development teams rarely include individuals with lived experience of marginalization.
- Design defaults cater to "normal" users, reinforcing exclusion.

4. Inadequate Testing Environments

- Products are tested in ideal conditions—urban offices, fast internet, literate users—not in the environments they claim to serve.

8.4 The Edge-Inward Design Philosophy

Instead of designing for the average and then "fixing" for the margins, Edge-Inward Design proposes:

Start with the most complex use case—and generalize outwards.

Benefits:

- Tools built for complexity can handle simplicity—but not vice versa.
- Design robustness increases. Error handling improves.
- System becomes more adaptable and user-configurable.
- Accessibility becomes a feature for all, not a patch for a few.

Example:

- AI keyboard for dyslexia with predictive correction, voice support, and emoji suggestions—later adopted by non-disabled users as a faster texting tool.

8.5 Case Study: Designing for Multilingual, Low-Literacy Rural Women

Background:

An NGO in Maharashtra co-designed a voice assistant for agricultural advice for rural women farmers who:

- Were non-literate
- Spoke a mix of dialects and local Marathi
- Had shared phones, limited privacy, and poor signal

Approach:

- Voice-first interaction, avoiding any text
- Trained on rural dialects, not just standard Marathi
- Included vernacular metaphors and local crops
- Supported asynchronous access—messages could be recorded offline and answered later
- Designed with user cooperatives, not for them

Outcomes:

- Tool usage was 5x higher than existing apps
- Led to the development of an offline version of the chatbot
- Inspired redesigns in other states using the same architecture

8.6 AI as Empowerment: Not Surveillance

Designing for the margins also means being wary of turning users into data subjects. In many low-income or disabled communities, AI becomes a tool of control—tracking, monitoring, correcting—rather than empowerment.

Examples of Harm:

- Facial recognition used in welfare schemes leading to exclusion.
- Eye tracking used to penalize "distracted" students with ADHD.
- Biometric authentication in ration systems failing due to poor fingerprint capture in disabled or elderly populations.

Guiding Principle:

Empower, don't discipline. Assist, don't replace. Respect, don't extract.

8.7 Recommendations for Inclusive AI Design

1. Start with edge cases in mind—not after the fact.
2. Co-design with people who will use the system.
3. Build for low-resource environments from the ground up.
4. Prioritize configurability and personalization.
5. Test in real-life, marginal contexts.
6. Balance data needs with dignity and privacy.
7. Educate designers and developers in disability theory, ethics, and inclusion.

Chapter 9: Building Accessible AI Teams and Culture

9.1 Introduction

Creating truly accessible AI systems requires more than just inclusive code—it demands inclusive creators. The journey toward inclusive technology begins long before the product lifecycle—it begins in recruitment rooms, team dynamics, and organizational values.

This chapter explores how accessibility can be embedded into the DNA of AI organizations, from hiring practices to daily workflows, and from physical infrastructure to inclusive leadership. A culture that embraces disability, neurodiversity, linguistic diversity, and intersectional identities doesn't just build better AI—it creates a new standard for ethical innovation.

9.2 The Accessibility Gap in AI Workplaces

Despite increased awareness about the need for diversity and inclusion in tech, disabled individuals remain drastically underrepresented in AI-related roles. Common systemic barriers include:

◈ **Inaccessible Recruitment Processes:**

- Online application portals incompatible with screen readers.
- Timed coding assessments disadvantaging neurodivergent applicants.

- Interview formats that emphasize social agility over technical depth.

◈ **Work Environment Challenges:**

- Office layouts that ignore mobility aids.
- Collaboration tools without captioning or screen reader support.
- Assumptions about constant availability and sensory regulation.

◈ **Cultural Exclusion:**

- Microaggressions and ableist language.
- Stereotyping of productivity and "professionalism."
- Isolation due to lack of mentorship for disabled talent.

Without proactive measures, even well-meaning organizations perpetuate environments that exclude the very communities their AI is supposed to serve.

9.3 Inclusive Hiring Practices

Rethinking the Entire Hiring Funnel

To build accessible AI teams, we must challenge every assumption embedded in hiring—from how we write job descriptions to how we measure talent.

📝 **Job Descriptions:**

- Use clear, plain language—avoiding idioms and vague expectations.

- Remove requirements not essential to the role (e.g., "excellent verbal skills" for backend roles).
- State availability of accommodations upfront to reduce applicant anxiety.

🧪 **Assessments**:

- Offer multiple ways to showcase skill: take-home projects, portfolio reviews, open-book code tests.
- Provide extra time or alternative formats (e.g., audio instead of written prompts).
- Normalize requests for accommodations by making them a visible part of the process.

💬 **Interviews**:

- Allow asynchronous video or written answers.
- Share questions ahead of time when possible.
- Train interviewers on bias, disability etiquette, and inclusive questioning.

🌐 **Outreach**:

- Collaborate with:
    - Disability-focused coding bootcamps.
    - University disability services offices.
    - NGOs focused on digital upskilling of disabled persons.
- Host accessibility-focused hackathons to spot untapped talent.

Inclusive hiring isn't about lowering the bar—it's about leveling the playing field.

9.4 Designing Accessible Workplaces

Workplaces that value accessibility move beyond basic compliance and actively support all types of bodies, minds, and learning styles.

A. Physical Accessibility:

- Adjustable desks, anti-glare lighting, accessible restrooms.
- Tactile navigation paths and braille signage.
- Seating zones for wheelchair access in all shared spaces.

B. Digital Accessibility:

- All internal tools should be screen reader compatible.
- Internal documentation should follow WCAG 2.1 guidelines.
- Automated alt-text generation for shared media.

C. Flexible Work Models:

- Embrace remote and hybrid options as defaults.
- Respect asynchronous communication—not everyone can attend meetings at 9am daily.
- Normalize flexible hours for people with chronic pain, fatigue, or caregiving duties.

D. Inclusive Communication Norms:

- Use captions in all meetings by default.

- Provide real-time chat transcripts.
- Encourage turn-taking, use of emojis for emotion signaling, and inclusive language guides.

E. Psychological Safety:

- Disable "camera-on" pressure in meetings.
- Allow quiet spaces and decompression time post-deadlines.
- Establish protocols for resolving ableism or microaggressions swiftly.

When accessibility becomes systemic and cultural, it empowers every team member to contribute fully.

9.5 Case Study: Building an Inclusive AI Lab from Scratch

Background:

The AI Research & Ethics Center in Bengaluru aimed to build the most inclusive AI lab in South Asia—hiring talent across disability spectrums, neurotypes, and linguistic minorities.

Initial Steps:

- Partnered with local NGOs like Enable India and Vidya Sagar to co-design onboarding flows.
- Allocated 15% of annual hiring slots to non-traditional applicants (dropouts, self-taught, disabled).
- Translated all internal documentation into Braille, Indian Sign Language (ISL), and simplified Hindi.

Operational Shifts:

- Weekly silent collaboration hours for deep work.
- Developed a custom Jupyter environment accessible via keyboard-only navigation and optimized for screen readers.
- Hosted monthly "Inclusion Sprints" where every team reviewed their deliverables from an accessibility lens.

Outcomes:

- Staff retention rose by 38%.
- Employee happiness scores averaged 9.3/10 in anonymous surveys.
- The lab received international funding for its work in AI-powered learning tools for neurodiverse children.

The case illustrates that inclusion, when embedded early, becomes a competitive advantage—not a burden.

9.6 Accessibility Champions and Internal Advocacy

The Role of Champions:

- Often volunteers or nominated leads who monitor accessibility within a team or org.
- Act as bridge-builders between users, developers, and leadership.
- Promote awareness, run workshops, and track progress via accessibility metrics.

Building a Champion Network:

- Start small—designate 1 champion per product area or business unit.
- Offer leadership training in inclusive design and disability rights.
- Recognize efforts through internal awards and performance metrics.

When accessibility advocacy becomes distributed, culture change accelerates organically.

9.7 Building Accessibility into Culture, Not Just Compliance

Accessibility must be value-driven, not rule-driven.

Compliance culture asks:

"What's the minimum I can do to meet this regulation?"

Accessibility culture asks:

"What can I do to make this better for *everyone*—now and in the future?"

Key Shifts:

- From "checklists" to co-creation with disabled users.
- From "fixing problems after launch" to embedding accessibility in design, testing, and deployment.
- From "legal liability" to ethical innovation.

Creating this culture requires buy-in from every level—executives to interns—and is sustained through stories, rituals, accountability, and visibility.

9.8 Recommendations for Organizations

Area	Action
Leadership	Embed accessibility KPIs in executive goals and reporting.
HR	Conduct an accessibility audit of hiring, onboarding, and retention.
Design	Implement inclusive design checklists and persona frameworks.
Engineering	Integrate accessibility testing into the CI/CD pipeline.
Policy	Offer mental health days, screen breaks, and adaptive leave.
Learning & Development	Provide mandatory training in digital accessibility and disability rights.
Outreach	Sponsor community initiatives, internships, and research in disability-inclusive AI.

Chapter 10: The Ethics of Co-Creation

10.1 Introduction

In the age of AI, ethical innovation demands more than theoretical frameworks—it calls for radical participation. Co-creation, at its core, is the practice of building with, not for, centering the voices and lived experiences of those traditionally excluded from technology design.

Especially in the context of accessibility, where AI can either empower or marginalize, co-creation is not optional—it's an ethical imperative.

This chapter explores the philosophical underpinnings, practical models, and critical responsibilities involved in co-creating ethical, accessible AI systems. It offers tools for moving from user-centered design to user-led innovation.

10.2 What is Co-Creation in the Context of AI?

Co-creation in AI refers to the collaborative process by which diverse stakeholders—especially marginalized and disabled communities—are actively involved in:

- Identifying the problem
- Shaping the research questions
- Defining success metrics
- Training, testing, and refining the models
- Evaluating outcomes and unintended consequences

Unlike traditional user research, which often extracts insights, co-creation builds reciprocal relationships where knowledge flows in both directions.

> "Nothing about us without us" is not just a slogan—it's a design principle.

10.3 Ethical Foundations of Co-Creation

Co-creation rests on a foundation of ethical pluralism, where multiple truths and lived realities are acknowledged and respected. Key ethical anchors include:

◈ **Justice and Redistribution**

- Prioritize communities who have been historically left out of tech benefits.
- Shift funding, power, and visibility toward marginalized creators.

◈ **Consent and Autonomy**

- Go beyond "informed consent" to ongoing, evolving consent.
- Let communities opt in and opt out of datasets, testing, and deployments.

◈ **Reciprocity**

- Compensate community members for their expertise and emotional labor.
- Ensure benefits (e.g., data insights, profits, tool access) flow back to contributors.

◈ **Transparency and Accountability**

- Co-develop feedback channels where users can challenge or modify AI behaviors.
- Publish impact statements detailing risks and trade-offs.

10.4 Models of Ethical Co-Creation

There is no one-size-fits-all blueprint, but several models have shown ethical robustness and scalability.

A. Participatory Action Research (PAR)

- Community members act as co-researchers, not just subjects.
- Emphasizes reflection-action cycles: test, reflect, iterate.

B. Value-Sensitive Design (VSD)

- Embeds ethical values into design requirements from the start.
- Helps navigate competing values like autonomy vs safety.

C. Community Technology Model

- Created by Detroit-based group Allied Media Projects.
- Focuses on slow tech development rooted in local culture, history, and needs.

D. Liberatory Design

- Developed by equity-focused educators and designers.

- Prioritizes healing, agency, and systemic disruption alongside usability.

These models move us from extraction to partnership, from problem-solving to power-sharing.

10.5 Case Study: ISL Dataset Co-Creation with Deaf Communities

Background:

An Indian startup aimed to build a deep learning model to recognize Indian Sign Language (ISL) gestures. Rather than scrape data or hire non-disabled annotators, they launched a community-centered co-creation initiative.

Steps Taken:

1. **Community Governance:**
    - Formed an advisory board with Deaf educators, ISL interpreters, and students.
    - Decided collectively on which signs to include, and how gestures would be framed.
2. **Participatory Data Collection:**
    - Held paid workshops where Deaf users performed signs in real conditions.
    - Captured variation in gesture style, speed, and expression.
3. **Ethical Consent Framework:**
    - Every contributor signed a modular consent form allowing opt-in for:
        - Academic research

        - Commercial use
        - Training only (not deployment)
    - Contributors retained rights to remove their data from future versions.
4. **Co-Modeling:**
    - Used an iterative loop:
        - Community gives feedback → Model adjusted → Retrained with new weights.
    - Invited community testers to evaluate bias and false positives.
5. **Reciprocity:**
    - Trained youth from Deaf schools to become AI literacy ambassadors.
    - Shared model results openly via an ISL-native web interface.
    - Community owns 20% of IP generated through licensing.

Outcome:

- Accuracy improved 12% over the baseline by using contextual gesture variation.
- Project became a model for AI ethics and dataset sovereignty in India.
- Inspired spin-off work in Marathi and Tamil sign language dialects.

This case highlights that co-creation is not slower—it's smarter, fairer, and more sustainable.

10.6 Power, Privilege, and Positionality

Any effort to co-create must interrogate the power dynamics involved.

Questions to Ask:

- Who is initiating this project? What is their positionality?
- Who has veto power, budget authority, or visibility?
- How do we ensure that the most affected communities have final say—not just advisory roles?

Practices to Address Power Imbalance:

- Share authorship and credit in publications and media.
- Build long-term relationships, not one-off engagements.
- Practice radical transparency in trade-offs, failures, and limits.

Accessibility co-creation is not neutral—it must be intentionally anti-oppressive.

10.7 Risks of Performative Co-Creation

Without integrity, co-creation can become performative, even extractive. Common pitfalls include:

- Tokenism: Involving one person from a marginalized group and calling it representation.

- Data Mining Disguised as Collaboration: Framing data extraction as "participation" with no feedback loop.
- Invisibility of Labor: Communities doing unpaid testing, labeling, or consulting with no acknowledgment.

Ethical co-creation requires accountability mechanisms, including:

- Grievance redressal pathways.
- Transparency dashboards.
- Community veto channels.

10.8 Ethical Frameworks and Tools for Teams

To operationalize co-creation ethics, teams can use:

Tool	Purpose
Ethical OS Toolkit	Anticipates unintended consequences of emerging tech.
AI Impact Assessment (AIIA)	Assesses societal and accessibility risks of AI systems.
Co-Creation Canvas	Plans stakeholders, power flow, compensation, and consent.

DSA Evaluation Matrix	Checks alignment with disability justice and rights frameworks.

These tools ensure ethics aren't theoretical—they're designed into every phase of AI development.

10.9 Conclusion

Ethical co-creation is not just a methodology—it's a mindset shift. It invites us to listen more, control less, and design with humility. When disabled communities, Indigenous groups, and neurodivergent innovators become co-owners of the AI future, we don't just make AI more inclusive—we make it more human.

> In the era of algorithmic dominance, the most radical thing we can do is co-create—with dignity, equity, and trust.

Chapter 11: Designing for Multilingual Accessibility in AI

11.1 Introduction

Inclusion in AI isn't just about functionality—it's about language, culture, and identity. For millions across the world, especially in linguistically diverse nations like India, accessibility begins with multilingual support.

Yet, many AI systems default to English or a few dominant languages, leaving regional and minority language speakers behind. True inclusivity in AI demands not only translation but cultural nuance, linguistic parity, and dialectal sensitivity.

This chapter explores the architectures, challenges, and innovations in building multilingual AI systems for accessibility—especially those that serve Deaf, low-literacy, neurodivergent, and non-native communities.

11.2 Why Multilingual Accessibility Matters

◆ Linguistic Inclusion is a Human Right

According to the UN Convention on the Rights of Persons with Disabilities (CRPD), access to information must be guaranteed in formats and languages appropriate to individual needs.

◆ AI Can Exclude by Default

English-centric datasets, models, and interfaces often lead to:

- Exclusion of non-native users from voice assistants.
- Misinterpretation in speech-to-text or NLP-based chatbots.
- Cultural erasure in AI-generated content or summaries.

◆ Multilingualism = Cultural Relevance

Language is not just a medium—it's a carrier of values, humor, idioms, and customs. Accessibility is incomplete without localization and contextual alignment.

11.3 Technical Foundations of Multilingual AI

Modern multilingual AI systems combine several components:

◆ Multilingual NLP Models

Large models like mBERT, XLM-R, and mT5 are trained on corpora spanning 100+ languages. These models can:

- Perform translation, summarization, and sentiment analysis.
- Understand context across languages using shared embedding spaces.

◆ Automatic Speech Recognition (ASR)

Multilingual ASR systems (e.g., Whisper, Google's LAS) convert spoken words into text across languages. Challenges include:

- Dialectal variation
- Low-resource phonetic diversity

- Code-switching (common in Indian speech)

◈ **Text-to-Speech (TTS) and Voice Cloning**

Voice engines now support multilingual TTS with regional accents and prosody modeling. Tools like Coqui, Mozilla TTS, and Descript Overdub bring synthetic speech closer to natural multilingual variation.

◈ **Multilingual OCR and Sign Recognition**

- OCR engines like Tesseract now support over 100 scripts (e.g., Devanagari, Tamil).
- Some sign recognition models incorporate regional dialects of sign languages, like Indian Sign Language (ISL) variations in Maharashtra or Tamil Nadu.

11.4 Challenges in Building Multilingual Accessible AI

Despite the progress, serious roadblocks remain:

1. Data Scarcity

- Many Indian and African languages are low-resource, lacking labeled corpora, speech recordings, or OCR datasets.

2. Script and Orthographic Diversity

- Indian languages alone use over 11 major scripts. Many models struggle to tokenize or align across different writing systems.

3. Dialects and Sociolects

- Language varies by region, caste, class, and gender. A model trained in "standard Hindi" may misinterpret rural dialects or Adivasi variants.

4. Code-Switching

- Common in everyday usage (e.g., "Main train se jaa raha hoon, please track check kar lo"), this confuses conventional NLP parsers.

5. Bias and Representation

- Multilingual corpora often overrepresent news, politics, or religious texts—but lack conversational, disability-focused, or youth-centered content.

11.5 Case Study: Creating a Marathi-English Bilingual AI Chatbot for Rural Accessibility

Background:

A grassroots NGO in Maharashtra partnered with a tech startup to build a bilingual chatbot to help Deaf and low-literacy farmers understand government schemes and weather forecasts.

Design Process:

1. **Community Interviews:**
   - Identified common words, slang, and abbreviations used in SMSes and speech.
   - Catalogued Marathi signs used by Deaf farmers alongside gesture-based explanations.
2. **Data Collection:**
   - Created a custom corpus using WhatsApp chats, local newspapers, and ISL-Marathi interpretations.

    - Used transliteration tools to capture Marathi typed in Latin script (e.g., "pani ahe ka?").

3. **Model Training:**
    - Fine-tuned mBERT with local text.
    - Built a Marathi-English intent classifier using rule-based fallback for low-confidence queries.

4. **Voice Integration:**
    - Integrated Marathi TTS for low-literacy users and video sign outputs for Deaf users.
    - Developed "tap-to-hear" and "tap-to-sign" features for every chatbot response.

5. **Iterative Feedback:**
    - Held monthly community testing rounds.
    - Added voice speed control, local slang toggles, and visual summaries for complex replies.

Outcome:

- Daily usage by 1,000+ users.
- 94% user satisfaction after three months.
- Inspired state-level pilots for other regions and languages.

This case illustrates that multilingual accessibility is not just a language task—it's an inclusive design effort.

11.6 Toward Equitable Multilingual Datasets

Without good data, good models are impossible. To enable ethical multilingual accessibility:

- Create community-led datasets (e.g., Bhojpuri folk songs, regional recipes, oral stories).
- Use crowdsourcing with ethical guardrails (fair pay, informed consent).
- Build translation pairs for sign + voice + text in each language.
- Involve local language teachers and linguists in labeling and annotation.

Open-sourcing these datasets under community licenses can shift control to the people who need it most.

11.7 Designing Interfaces for Multilingual Access

Beyond the models, the UI/UX layer must support linguistic diversity:

- Language toggles with icon + native script
- Local script input fields with IME support
- Audio or sign-language responses
- Context-sensitive translation (e.g., agriculture-specific Marathi terms vs generic)
- Low-literacy modes: emojis, icons, voice-first design

Building inclusive language experiences means designing for more than just translation—it means designing for dignity.

11.8 Conclusion: Multilingual AI as Accessibility Infrastructure

When we treat multilingualism as an accessibility requirement, not a feature, we unlock innovation that is more inclusive, democratic, and human-centered.

Multilingual AI is not just about reaching more users—it's about representing more realities, preserving cultural identity, and amplifying the voices of the underserved.

> In a world of monolingual machines, designing for multilingual accessibility is an act of justice.

Chapter 12: Policies and Frameworks for AI Accessibility

12.1 Introduction

Creating accessible AI is not just a technical or ethical ambition—it is a legal and societal obligation. Governments, tech companies, and civil society must work together within structured policies and governance models to ensure that AI technologies are inclusive by design.

This chapter explores the international frameworks, national policies, and industry standards that shape the landscape of AI accessibility. It also highlights the gaps, challenges, and opportunities in creating a robust policy ecosystem that supports people with disabilities, linguistic minorities, and neurodiverse communities.

12.2 The Legal Foundations of Accessibility

◈ The UN Convention on the Rights of Persons with Disabilities (CRPD)

- Adopted in 2006, ratified by 185+ countries.
- Mandates accessible ICTs and equal access to digital environments.
- Recognizes sign language and alternative communication as equal to spoken language.
- Supports innovation that empowers disabled persons' autonomy and participation.

◈ **The Web Content Accessibility Guidelines (WCAG)**

- Developed by the W3C, WCAG is the gold standard for digital accessibility.
- Principles: Perceivable, Operable, Understandable, and Robust (POUR).
- Though not AI-specific, these guidelines are being adapted for AI-driven interfaces, chatbots, and dynamic content.

◈ **The Marrakesh Treaty (2013)**

- Focuses on the accessibility of published works for the visually impaired.
- Encourages accessible digital formats via AI-driven conversion tools (e.g., OCR, TTS, braille rendering).

12.3 National Policies and Initiatives

India: Accessible India Campaign (Sugamya Bharat Abhiyan)

- Focuses on digital, transport, and infrastructure accessibility.
- Promotes accessible websites and government services, but lacks AI-specific policy language.

United States: Americans with Disabilities Act (ADA)

- Courts are increasingly interpreting ADA to include digital platforms.
- AI-powered services (e.g., hiring bots, educational tools) must not discriminate.

EU: European Accessibility Act (EAA)

- Mandates accessibility in banking, e-commerce, education, and telecom services by 2025.
- Covers voice assistants, chatbots, and AI interfaces used in public services.

Canada: Accessible Canada Act

- A forward-looking law that explicitly names AI systems in accessibility contexts.
- Includes funding for inclusive AI research and community-driven design.

12.4 Rights for Person with Disabilities Act ,2016 - India

Empowering 21st Century India through Inclusion and Accessibility

🔍 Overview

The Rights of Persons with Disabilities Act, 2016 is a landmark legislation that replaced the Persons with Disabilities (Equal Opportunities, Protection of Rights and Full Participation) Act, 1995. Enacted to align Indian law with the UN Convention on the Rights of Persons with Disabilities (UNCRPD), the RPWD Act marks a decisive shift from a medical and charity-based model to a rights-based and inclusive approach to disability.

🆚 1995 vs. 2016: What Changed?

Aspect	1995 Act	2016 Act
Disabilities Covered	7 categories	Expanded to 21 categories, including new ones

		like autism, thalassemia, and acid attack victims
Approach	Welfare-based / medical model	Rights-based, inclusive, and equality-driven
Reservation in Jobs	3% for PWDs	4% reservation for persons with benchmark disabilities
Education	Basic mention of education	Free & inclusive education guaranteed from age 6–18, 5% reservation in higher education
Legal Capacity	Limited, paternalistic provisions	Full legal recognition & decision-making support for persons with disabilities
Accessibility	Limited scope	Mandatory universal accessibility in physical and digital infrastructure

Penalties for Violations	No specific punitive measures	Criminal penalties for discrimination, abuse, or denial of rights
Implementation	Central Coordination Committee	Institutional bodies: Chief Commissioner, State Commissioners, District Committees

🔑 Key Provisions of RPWD Act, 2016

◆ Expanded List of Disabilities (21 Total) includes:

- Autism Spectrum Disorder
- Cerebral Palsy
- Multiple Sclerosis
- Muscular Dystrophy
- Mental Illness
- Specific Learning Disabilities
- Speech and Language Disability
- Acid Attack Victims
- Hemophilia, Thalassemia, Sickle Cell Disease, and more

◆ Education Rights

- Free, inclusive education for ages 6–18

- 5% reservation in higher educational institutions
- Provisions for accessible learning materials and assistive technologies

◆ Employment Provisions

- 4% reservation in government jobs
- Non-discrimination in hiring, promotions, and training
- Establishments must appoint a Liaison Officer for disability inclusion

◆ Accessibility

- Mandates barrier-free access in public buildings, transport, and ICT
- Includes deadlines for retrofitting and compliance

◆ Legal Recognition & Protection

- Recognizes equal legal capacity for persons with disabilities
- Provides for limited guardianship where necessary
- Strict penalties for harassment, abuse, or discrimination

◆ Grievance Redressal & Implementation

- Establishes:
- Chief Commissioner for Persons with Disabilities (National)

- State Commissioners
- District-level Committees
- Advisory Boards to monitor and enforce the Act

🧭 **Why It Matters**

The RPWD Act, 2016 is a transformative law in India that recognizes disability as a part of human diversity. It empowers persons with disabilities to live with dignity, participate fully in society, and access opportunities on an equal basis with others.

12.5 Industry Standards and Guidelines for Accessible AI

Beyond laws, tech companies and international bodies have begun defining accessibility guidelines specific to AI systems.

◈ **ISO/IEC TR 24028 (Trustworthiness in AI)**

- Describes accessibility as a trust component in AI.
- Suggests multimodal interfaces and user feedback loops.

◈ **G3ict and ITU's AI4A Guidelines**

- Developed with disabled users in mind.
- Promote:
    - Captioning, sign output, TTS in multiple languages
    - Compatibility with assistive devices
    - Customizable speed, layout, and control

◈ **Microsoft's Inclusive Design Toolkit**

- Offers checklists for designers and engineers:
    - Keyboard navigation for AI dashboards
    - Color-blind safe data visualizations
    - Cognitive load testing for AI recommendations

◈ **Apple and Google Accessibility APIs**

- Enable developers to embed screen reader labels, ARIA tags, and voice control natively into AI apps.
- AI voice agents (e.g., Siri, Google Assistant) now support multiple languages, accents, and simplified mode switches.

12.6 Gaps in Current Policy Landscapes

Despite progress, policy frameworks still lag behind AI innovation, especially in accessibility:

Area	Current State	Needed Direction
Sign Language in AI	Rarely covered in regulations	Recognition of regional sign dialects
Cognitive Accessibility	Lacks global guidelines	AI testing with neurodiverse users
Multilingual AI Standards	Fragmented or absent	Benchmarks for regional

		language support
Data Governance	Often generic	Disability-sensitive data policies
Procurement Regulations	Don't enforce accessible AI requirements	Mandate inclusive design in public tools

12.7 Case Study: AI Accessibility Policy Reform in Canada

Background:

In 2022, the Canadian Digital Accessibility Bill (C-22) included a special focus on AI in public services.

Approach:

- Formed a Disability & AI Task Force with activists, developers, and legal scholars.
- Piloted accessibility scoring for AI tools used in immigration, education, and welfare.
- Adopted WCAG + AI-specific metrics: screen reader compatibility, TTS quality, and voice assistant bias detection.

Result:

- By 2024, over 70% of public-facing AI tools had passed independent accessibility audits.
- Canada became the first country to fund regional AI sign datasets and multilingual testing labs.

12.8 Toward Global Alignment

A unified global policy ecosystem for accessible AI could include:

◈ **Accessibility AI Benchmarking Consortium**

- Shared global tests for multilingual TTS, ISL recognition, cognitive adaptation.

◆ **UN Accessibility AI Charter**

- Commitments from governments and tech giants to:
    - Open-source inclusive datasets
    - Involve disabled people in product development
    - Report AI accessibility metrics annually

◈ **Public Procurement Standards**

- Governments could demand accessibility scoring (like WCAG conformance) for all AI tools in public contracts.

12.9 Conclusion: Policy as Infrastructure for Justice

Laws and policies are not just compliance mechanisms—they are infrastructures for equity.

As AI increasingly mediates access to healthcare, education, employment, and social participation, accessibility must be embedded in law, not left to goodwill.

> "When accessibility becomes a legal expectation, not a post-launch patch, AI systems evolve into tools for justice—not just convenience."

Chapter 13: AI for Accessibility in Education

13.1 Introduction

Education is a universal right, yet for millions of students with disabilities, the system remains far from inclusive. Inaccessible classrooms, rigid teaching methods, and non-adaptive evaluation systems compound systemic exclusion. Fortunately, Artificial Intelligence (AI) has emerged as a powerful equalizer—capable of transforming educational spaces into flexible, personalized, and inclusive ecosystems.

This chapter explores how AI can bridge accessibility gaps in education by examining key applications, design principles, implementation strategies, and real-world deployments across diverse learning environments.

13.2 Barriers to Accessible Education

Before we explore solutions, it's essential to understand the depth of challenges:

◆ Physical Barriers

- Inaccessible infrastructure in schools (ramps, lifts, classrooms)
- Non-adaptive learning materials for students with low vision or hearing loss

◇ Cognitive and Learning Challenges

- Rigid curricula that don't accommodate neurodiverse learners

- Standardized testing systems unsuited for non-verbal or dyslexic students

❖ **Language and Communication Gaps**

- Lack of Indian Sign Language (ISL) support in classrooms
- Monolingual platforms that exclude regional language learners

❖ **Teacher Training and Awareness**

- Most educators lack training in inclusive teaching methods
- Misunderstanding or underestimation of student capabilities

13.3 The Role of AI in Transforming Learning Environments

AI can help dismantle these barriers through adaptive, real-time, and personalized solutions:

❖ **Multimodal Learning**

AI systems offer content in visual, auditory, and textual forms:

- Speech-to-text for deaf students
- Text-to-speech for visually impaired learners
- Video content with real-time ISL translation

❖ **Personalized Learning Pathways**

- AI tutors adjust content difficulty, pacing, and format based on student performance and preferences

- Tools like Microsoft's Immersive Reader adapt content for dyslexic or ADHD learners

◈ **Real-Time Feedback**

- AI-driven quizzes offer instant feedback with explanations
- Gesture-recognition systems detect confusion, distraction, or frustration

13.4 AI Tools for Inclusive Classrooms

◈ 1. AI-Powered Captioning and Translation

- Google's Live Transcribe or Microsoft Translator enable real-time classroom captioning
- Platforms like Ava provide multilingual, multi-speaker captioning for group discussions

◈ 2. Sign Language Recognition and Synthesis

- Deep learning models interpret sign gestures from students and synthesize ISL responses
- Tools like SignAll and ISL-recognition prototypes use computer vision + NLP

◈ 3. Intelligent Tutoring Systems

- Tools like Carnegie Learning and Squirrel AI track cognitive load and personalize content delivery
- OpenAI-based chatbots support Q&A in local languages with contextual understanding

◈ 4. Emotion-Aware Systems

- AI systems like Affectiva detect facial cues to gauge student engagement
- Adjusts teaching strategies in real-time for shy, anxious, or inattentive students

13.5 Case Studies: AI Empowering Inclusive Education

Case Study 1: Avaz – India's Pioneering AAC App for Non-Verbal Children

Background:

In India, children with non-verbal communication disabilities such as autism spectrum disorder (ASD), cerebral palsy, and Down syndrome often face exclusion from mainstream classrooms due to a lack of appropriate communication aids. Recognizing this gap, Invention Labs (a Chennai-based startup) developed *Avaz*—an Augmentative and Alternative Communication (AAC) app that leverages AI to empower non-verbal users.

How AI Powers Avaz:

- Predictive Vocabulary Suggestion: The app uses NLP-based models to learn communication patterns and offer relevant words/phrases in real-time.
- Image-to-Word Association: For children who respond better to visuals, the app uses AI to map images with frequently used phrases (adaptive learning).
- Multi-language Support: Avaz's AI engine is trained to switch across multiple Indian

languages and dialects, enabling regional language support.

- Voice Customization: Speech synthesis adapts based on the child's preference for pitch, gender, and speed.

Impact:

- Over 100,000 downloads, adopted in special education classrooms across India and Southeast Asia.
- Reported improvement in literacy, social participation, and emotional expression among early users.
- Integrated with government-run inclusive education programs in Tamil Nadu and Maharashtra.

Challenges:

- Requires smartphones/tablets, which limits reach in low-income rural areas.
- Needs continual dataset refinement to accommodate regional symbol-language mappings.

Case Study 2: Microsoft Reading Progress – Dyslexia-Aware Learning Analytics

Background:

Traditional reading fluency assessments are stressful for dyslexic learners due to time pressure, judgment, and lack of individualized feedback. Microsoft Education introduced *Reading Progress*—an AI-based reading assistant that allows students to practice reading aloud independently.

AI Capabilities:

- Speech Recognition with Phoneme-Level Accuracy: Detects substitutions, omissions, mispronunciations, and hesitations.
- Progress Analytics: Tracks reading speed, accuracy, and word difficulty over time to personalize support.
- Teacher Dashboard: Automatically flags problem areas for teacher review, allowing customized intervention plans.

Innovation:

- Trained on datasets that include non-native English speakers and dyslexic reading styles, reducing bias.
- Offers customizable reading texts, genres, and complexity levels per learner.
- Integrates into Microsoft Teams, making it accessible across hybrid learning environments.

Impact:

- Over 1.5 million students in 23 countries have used the tool.
- Reports show increased reading confidence and reduced reading anxiety.

- Significant uptake in inclusive education programs in the U.S., Australia, and India (via Azure-supported pilots).

Challenges:

- Relies heavily on English content—support for Indian regional languages is in beta.
- Requires internet connectivity for full feature access.

🧩 Case Study 3: ISL Recognition Research - IIT Delhi's Sign Language Dataset

Background:

The absence of large-scale Indian Sign Language (ISL) datasets has historically hindered the development of AI models for ISL recognition and translation. IIT Delhi, in collaboration with the Ministry of Social Justice, initiated a pioneering effort to build a diverse, annotated ISL video dataset for machine learning research.

AI Focus:

- Computer Vision for Gesture Recognition: CNN + RNN architectures trained on over 10,000 gesture video clips.
- Pose Estimation Algorithms: 3D skeletal modeling using MediaPipe and OpenPose to analyze finger and hand movement.
- Language Mapping Engine: NLP-based sequence prediction translates ISL gestures into grammatically correct Hindi/English text.

Applications Built on the Dataset:

- AI-based ISL translators embedded in EdTech tools
- Educational chatbots that support deaf users with text-based responses
- ISL-to-speech pilot projects in vocational training centers

Impact:

- Enabled the first ISL interpreter prototype for digital classrooms
- Used in training over 5,000 teachers and 50+ NGOs
- Recognized as a national benchmark in inclusive AI research

Challenges:

- Many regional dialects of ISL remain underrepresented
- Gesture detection accuracy drops in low-light or cluttered environments

🧩 Case Study 4: Cognify – Adaptive Learning for Neurodiverse Students (Australia)

Background:

Cognify, developed by ACER (Australian Council for Educational Research), addresses the lack of dynamic learning environments for students with ADHD, dyslexia, and other neurodevelopmental disorders. The tool uses reinforcement learning and cognitive profiling to adapt content in real time.

AI Mechanisms:

- User Profiling Engine: Builds cognitive profiles using initial assessment games, response times, and emotional cues.
- RL-based Adaptive Pacing: Learns optimal challenge levels per student and adjusts question complexity accordingly.
- Gamified Learning Interface: Combines behavioral psychology with AI to maintain motivation and engagement.

Outcomes:

- Used in over 400 inclusive schools across Australia, New Zealand, and pilot locations in India.
- Improved retention and concept mastery rates by over 30% in neurodiverse learners.
- Cited in academic journals as a benchmark for emotion-aware pedagogy.

Challenges:

- Requires continuous A/B testing to avoid over-adaptation (which can hinder learning stretch)
- Still under development for multilingual deployments in South Asia

13.6 Implementation Challenges in India

While promising, the road to AI-driven inclusive education in India faces hurdles:

◆ **Infrastructure Gaps**

- Limited internet access and outdated hardware in rural schools
- Lack of assistive devices in public education

◆ **Teacher Resistance or Lack of Training**

- Limited digital literacy among teachers
- Perception of AI as a threat rather than a tool

◆ **Data Privacy Concerns**

- AI requires collecting and analyzing student behavior, raising consent and data security concerns

◆ **Bias in Datasets**

- AI tools trained on Western contexts often misinterpret Indian accents, cultural expressions, or local ISL variations

13.7 Designing AI for Inclusive Education: Key Principles

1. Universal Design for Learning (UDL)

- Design curriculum with multiple means of representation, expression, and engagement

2. Low-Tech Adaptability

- Ensure tools work offline or with minimal data consumption

- Include SMS or USSD-based interactions for underserved regions

3. Multilingual, Multicultural Sensitivity

- Support Indian languages, dialects, and regional educational styles

4. Student-Led Feedback Loops

- Allow learners to modify pace, request clarification, or submit feedback

13.8 Future of AI in Education Accessibility

◈ On-Device AI Tutors

- Portable AI tutors that function without internet—ideal for rural and tribal areas

◆ Inclusive AR/VR for Special Education

- Immersive, accessible virtual learning environments for students with mobility or cognitive impairments

◈ Federated Learning for Student Privacy

- Models trained on-device, ensuring data never leaves the student's device

◈ Emotionally Adaptive Curricula

- Real-time curriculum adaptation based on fatigue, frustration, or confidence levels

13.9 Conclusion: From Smart Classrooms to Smart Equality

AI offers the potential to redefine education not just as a system—but as an equalizer. When thoughtfully designed and equitably deployed, AI tools can do more than just teach—they can see, listen, understand, and respond to every learner's unique needs.

To build such a future, we must combine AI innovation with policy reform, teacher empowerment, and deep collaboration with the disabled community.

> ***"Inclusive education is not a feature—it is the foundation of a just and intelligent society."***

Chapter 14: India's Journey Toward Digital Accessibility: Policies, Programs, and Real-World Case Studies

Digital accessibility in India has evolved from a fringe consideration into a national development imperative. While laws like the Rights of Persons with Disabilities (RPwD) Act provide the legal foundation, it is the policies, programs, and practical initiatives that have driven large-scale change. India's socio-cultural diversity, multilingualism, and digital divide pose unique challenges – yet innovation and inclusion are steadily becoming core pillars of digital transformation across government and industry. This chapter outlines key national efforts and real-world case studies that illustrate India's roadmap to a digitally accessible future.

National Policies and Programs Promoting Digital Accessibility

14.1 Accessible India Campaign (Sugamya Bharat Abhiyan)

Launched in 2015, this flagship initiative aims to make both physical and digital environments barrier-free. Key digital accessibility goals include:

- Auditing and remediating over 900 government websites.
- Promoting the creation of accessible public apps.
- Training IT personnel and web developers on accessibility standards.

14.2 National Policy on Universal Electronic Accessibility (2013)

This policy was the first step toward mainstreaming digital inclusion in electronics and ICT. It advocated for:

- Accessible design as a default in public procurement.
- Research and development in Indian assistive technologies.
- Localization of tools and platforms for wider access.

14.3 Digital India Programme

Accessibility is a built-in objective under this nationwide digitization initiative. Key actions include:

- Making major apps (UMANG, DigiLocker, MyGov) screen reader compatible.
- Providing text-to-speech and voice input in multiple Indian languages.
- Developing accessibility checklists for app and web development teams.

14.4 Guidelines for Indian Government Websites (GIGW 3.0)

GIGW ensures that government websites and apps:

- Comply with WCAG 2.1 Level AA standards.
- Support accessible PDF documents and keyboard-only navigation.
- Are tested with real users with disabilities before launch.

14.5 Digital Saksharta Abhiyan (DISHA)

This digital literacy program integrates accessibility by:

- Training community workers to assist persons with disabilities.
- Distributing assistive software in local languages.
- Teaching basic ICT skills to visually impaired and low-literacy users.

14.6 Bureau of Indian Standards (BIS) IS 17802:2023

India's new accessibility standard harmonizes with WCAG guidelines and serves as a benchmark for accessible design in public-facing ICT systems.

Real-World Case Studies: Inclusion in Action

14.7 Case Study : NIC's Website Accessibility Overhaul

- The National Informatics Centre worked with central ministries to make their websites accessible.
- Focus on ALT text, skip links, high contrast, and screen reader compatibility.
- Resulted in improved usability for visually impaired and keyboard-only users.

14.8 Case Study : DAISY India & Saksham Trust

- Digitized over 50,000 textbooks in accessible formats (DAISY, EPUB, Braille).
- Distributed via *Sugamya Pustakalaya*, India's first accessible online library.

- Empowered blind students across states to access the same learning material as peers.

14.9 Case Study : XRCVC's Financial Accessibility Campaign

- Partnered with banks to ensure their digital banking platforms are accessible.
- Trained users with vision impairments to use UPI, BHIM, and mobile banking apps.
- Pushed for talking ATMs and inclusive biometric devices.

14.10 Case Study : Microsoft India – AI for Accessibility

- Supported startups working on ISL recognition, AI tools for dyslexia, and smart screen readers.
- Promoted inclusive product design in education, communication, and health.

14.11 Case Study : TCS' Digital Accessibility Model

- Internally enforced WCAG compliance for all products.
- Employed persons with disabilities as accessibility testers.
- Partnered with NGOs to train underrepresented groups for digital jobs.

14.12 Case Study: Kerala's Sutherland Digital Accessibility Centre

- First government-private testing center where persons with disabilities audit government apps and websites.
- Over 200 platforms improved in terms of accessibility.
- Created local employment and awareness.

14.13 Case Study: e-Pathshala by NCERT

- Introduced audio textbooks, screen reader compatibility, and font scaling.
- Local language support in 22+ languages for multilingual accessibility.
- Widely used during COVID-19 to support inclusive online learning.

14.14 Case Study: Reserve Bank of India's Push for Accessible Banking

- All banks directed to ensure accessibility in apps and net banking.
- SBI and HDFC released apps tested for NVDA and TalkBack.
- Braille features and voice interfaces introduced in many ATMs.

14.15 Case Study: Startups under Startup India & Accessible Tech

- Thinkerbell Labs created *Annie*, the world's first Braille self-learning device.

- Trestle Labs built tools to convert printed text to audio and Braille in real time.
- InSign Language developed sign language avatars for digital content translation.

14.16 Case Study: CDAC's e-Governance Accessibility Toolkit

- Provided automated and manual accessibility testing tools.
- Used by states like Maharashtra and Karnataka to fix e-district portals.
- Included protocols for user-centered design and multilingual content.

14.17 Case Study: Inclusys Foundation's Accessibility Bootcamps

- Conducted digital skill-building camps for the hearing and mobility impaired.
- Taught use of NVDA, Google Live Transcribe, Ava, and AI-based visual recognition tools.
- Focus on employability and independence in digital contexts.

14.18 Case Study: IIT Madras' Vaani Project

- Developed an Indian Sign Language to text converter using AI.
- Piloted in special schools and online learning platforms.
- Targeted toward making education and public services more inclusive.

14.19 Case Study: Election Commission's Accessible Voting App

- App included audio guidance, ISL videos, and high-contrast UI.
- SMS-based registration for the deaf.
- First time many users with disabilities could independently vote using digital tools.

Conclusion: Toward an Accessible Digital Bharat

India's digital accessibility landscape is being reshaped by a unique blend of public policy, technological innovation, grassroots action, and user-driven design. From screen-reader-ready educational platforms to accessible banking, and from inclusive entrepreneurship to AI-powered assistive tools, the momentum is clear.

As we move forward, scaling these initiatives, investing in capacity building, and embedding accessibility into every stage of digital product development will be critical. India's digital transformation must continue to include every citizen – regardless of disability, language, or location – to truly build an Accessible Bharat.

Chapter 15: Building for Neurodiverse Users

15.1 Introduction

Neurodiversity refers to the natural variation in the human brain that affects learning, attention, social interaction, and information processing. It includes individuals with autism spectrum disorder (ASD), attention deficit hyperactivity disorder (ADHD), dyslexia, dyspraxia, and other cognitive differences.

Building AI systems for neurodiverse users is not just about accommodation—it's about celebrating diversity and designing for multiple modes of interaction, perception, and cognition. AI can adapt interfaces, content delivery, and communication styles to support neurodiverse individuals across education, employment, and everyday digital experiences.

15.2 Who Are Neurodiverse Users?

Neurodiverse users may:

- Process information visually, verbally, or through tactile engagement.
- Prefer consistent, predictable interfaces.
- Experience sensory overload with bright lights, loud sounds, or cluttered screens.
- Face challenges with executive function (e.g., organizing tasks, time management).

- Have extraordinary attention to detail, memory, or pattern recognition.

Key groups include:

- Autistic individuals
- People with ADHD
- Dyslexic and dyspraxic users
- Tourette's syndrome
- Highly sensitive persons (HSP)

15.3 Challenges Faced in Digital Systems

1. **Sensory Overload**
    - Flashing elements, complex animations, and pop-up interactions can cause stress or confusion.
2. **Unclear Instructions**
    - Interfaces that rely on metaphors or ambiguous commands can confuse users with literal interpretation styles.
3. **Executive Dysfunction**
    - Multi-step processes, inconsistent navigation, or cluttered layouts can hinder task completion.
4. **Lack of Customization**
    - One-size-fits-all design does not accommodate varying cognitive and perceptual preferences.

5. **Unintentional Exclusion**

    - AI systems that rely on sentiment analysis, facial emotion detection, or social cues may misinterpret neurodiverse users.

15.4 Principles of Inclusive Design for Neurodiversity

1. Clarity and Simplicity

- Use straightforward language.
- Keep layout consistent and predictable.
- Break down tasks into manageable chunks.

2. Customizability

- Let users control color schemes, font sizes, animation speeds, and sound levels.
- Provide options for text vs. voice vs. image-based interfaces.

3. Low Cognitive Load

- Minimize distractions and avoid clutter.
- Offer focused modes (e.g., only showing one step at a time).

4. Support Emotional and Social Differences

- Avoid interfaces that rely heavily on sarcasm, irony, or facial expressions.
- Offer alternative communication channels (e.g., chatbots instead of video calls).

15.5 Case Study: Microsoft's Inclusive Design for Autism

Background: Microsoft has been a pioneer in neurodiverse hiring and design. Their Inclusive Design Toolkit emphasizes accessibility for people with cognitive and sensory differences.

Highlights:

- Surface Devices and Windows Accessibility Settings:
  - Users can turn off animations, simplify UI, and personalize input methods.
- **Microsoft Teams:**
  - "Together Mode" reduces visual clutter in video calls.
  - Background blur options reduce distractions.
- **Hiring Program for Autism:**
  - Tailors interview processes to reduce anxiety, allowing candidates to demonstrate technical skills without traditional interviews.

Impact:

- Higher retention and job satisfaction among neurodiverse employees.
- A user base that benefits from clearer design, not just neurodiverse individuals.

15.6 Case Study: CogniXR – Personalized Learning for Dyslexia and ADHD

Overview: CogniXR is an AI-powered edtech startup that builds adaptive learning platforms for children with dyslexia, ADHD, and other neurodivergences.

How it Works:

- Uses eye-tracking and neural feedback to gauge attention.
- AI adjusts content complexity, font types (e.g., OpenDyslexic), pacing, and format.
- Real-time analytics flag moments of disengagement, offering visual or auditory redirection.

Technical Stack:

- Reinforcement learning to adapt teaching style over time.
- Natural language understanding to simplify complex sentences for easier comprehension.
- Gamified interaction models to boost engagement for ADHD learners.

Results:

- 34% increase in task retention among ADHD users.
- 27% faster reading times in dyslexic learners after 6 weeks.

15.7 Building AI Systems That Embrace Neurodiversity

1. Training AI with Diverse Data

- Facial expression and sentiment models must include neurodiverse faces and interpretations.
- Text sentiment analysis should avoid over-reliance on tone or structure that may be different in neurodiverse communication.

2. Context-Aware Personalization

- AI systems should adapt based on usage patterns:
    - If a user often rewinds video instructions, the system could slow default playback.
    - If a user prefers keyboard over mouse, AI can recommend shortcuts.

3. Ethical Considerations

- Do not label or profile users based on neurodiversity.
- Maintain user control over customization settings.
- Avoid using AI to "normalize" neurodiverse behavior; aim for support, not correction.

15.8 Tools and Resources for Designers and Developers

- W3C Cognitive Accessibility Roadmap
- Microsoft Inclusive Design Toolkit
- GOV.UK Accessibility Guidelines for Neurodiverse Users
- Chrome Extensions:

    - *BeeLine Reader* (focus aid)
    - *Mercury Reader* (distraction-free reading)
- Design Systems:
    - Adobe Spectrum, Google Material Design – with built-in accessibility frameworks

15.9 Toward Neurodiverse-Centered AI Design

As AI continues to shape our digital environments, it must evolve beyond accessibility checklists and toward neurodiverse-centered design. Neurodiverse individuals offer unique ways of interacting with the world, and AI should support—rather than marginalize—those modes of engagement.

> ***Neurodiversity is not a challenge to be fixed, but a lens through which more empathetic, adaptable, and human AI systems can be built.***

Chapter 16: AI and Accessibility in Remote Work Environments

16.1 Introduction

The COVID-19 pandemic accelerated the adoption of remote work globally, but for persons with disabilities, the shift was both an opportunity and a challenge. Remote work dismantled many physical barriers—such as inaccessible office buildings and commuting—but it also exposed new digital accessibility gaps. In this chapter, we explore how Artificial Intelligence (AI) is transforming remote work environments into more inclusive spaces, enabling people with diverse abilities to collaborate, communicate, and contribute effectively from anywhere.

16.2 The Accessibility Challenges in Remote Work

Remote work creates its own accessibility issues:

- Communication Barriers
- Video conferencing platforms may lack real-time captions or support for sign language interpreters.
- Digital Fatigue and Cognitive Overload
- Back-to-back virtual meetings and multitasking requirements strain neurodiverse users and those with chronic fatigue.
- Inaccessible Productivity Tools

- Not all project management or collaboration tools are compatible with screen readers or accessible navigation patterns.
- Lack of Assistive Tech Integration
- Many remote platforms do not integrate well with assistive technologies like voice input systems or switch controls.

16.3 How AI Enhances Accessibility in Remote Work

1. Real-Time Transcription and Captioning

AI-driven speech recognition converts spoken words into on-screen captions in real time. Tools like Otter.ai, Zoom's live transcription, and Google Meet's captions enable deaf and hard-of-hearing users to participate independently.

2. Language Translation

Automatic translation allows global teams to collaborate, and enables deaf users who use sign language as their first language to follow English-centric discussions more easily.

3. AI-Based Scheduling Assistants

AI assistants like Microsoft Cortana or x.ai can manage meeting times, recommend breaks, and prevent cognitive overload by spacing out tasks.

4. Natural Language Processing for Summarization

AI tools can summarize long threads in chats or emails, helping neurodiverse individuals or those with cognitive disabilities focus on essentials.

5. Emotion-Aware AI Systems

AI can detect signs of stress, fatigue, or disengagement during meetings and prompt nudges such as "take a break" or "switch to focus mode."

16.4 Case Study: Google Workspace and Accessibility-First AI

Background: Google integrated accessibility features into Google Workspace to support inclusive collaboration in education and workplaces.

Key Features:

- Google Docs Voice Typing for motor-disabled users.
- AI-Powered Grammar Suggestions support users with dyslexia.
- Smart Compose in Gmail reduces typing effort for users with repetitive strain injuries or cognitive delays.
- Google Meet:
    - Auto-captions in multiple languages
    - Spotlight mode for visual tracking
    - Keyboard-based navigation

Outcome: Organizations with diverse teams reported higher engagement and reduced isolation for employees with disabilities, especially during prolonged periods of remote work.

16.5 Case Study: AccessiBee for Enterprise Collaboration Platforms

Background: AccessiBee develops AI-powered solutions that retrofit accessibility into existing platforms like Slack, Notion, Trello, and Jira.

Functionality:

- *Overlays for screen reader support in real-time messaging apps*
- *Voice-command plugins for Trello cards and Notion pages*
- *Personalized UI rendering based on user disability profiles*

Technical Stack:

- Reinforcement learning agents adapt to user navigation habits
- Dynamic content recognition ensures new updates stay accessible

Result: Employees with cognitive and visual impairments reported a 42% increase in ease-of-use when working with project management tools. HR departments noted higher participation in asynchronous collaboration.

16.6 Designing AI for Inclusive Remote Workflows

1. Context-Aware Collaboration

AI systems can adapt communication formats based on user profiles—for instance, converting voice notes to text summaries for hearing-impaired users.

2. AI-Powered Accessibility Dashboards

Dashboards can monitor accessibility compliance in shared documents, presentations, or team folders—flagging missing alt text, bad color contrast, or illegible fonts.

3. Smart Meeting Tools

Features such as:

- Emotion detection to reduce burnout
- Background blur and simplification for focus
- Text-to-speech summaries after each meeting

4. Virtual Co-Pilot Systems

These digital assistants can:

- Guide neurodiverse users through task sequences
- Suggest optimized routines
- Offer real-time nudges when distraction or confusion is detected

16.7 Security and Privacy Implications

Remote AI accessibility tools often require continuous data capture—from voice to video to emotional state. This raises key concerns:

- Consent Management: AI tools must obtain explicit and informed consent.
- Data Minimization: Only necessary data should be collected, and it should be anonymized.
- Edge AI: On-device processing for accessibility tools can limit data exposure and increase trust.

16.8 The Future: Hybrid Work with AI-Augmented Accessibility

The future of work is hybrid, and AI will be instrumental in blending physical and virtual spaces with inclusivity at the core. Expect to see:

- AI-powered AR glasses providing real-time captioning and navigation.
- Virtual whiteboards with haptic feedback for blind or low-vision users.
- Personalized digital workspaces that adjust to individual neurocognitive needs automatically.

16.9 Key Takeaways

- AI can dismantle digital barriers in remote and hybrid workspaces by offering adaptive, personalized, and real-time support.
- Collaboration platforms must integrate accessibility features natively—not as afterthoughts.
- The best AI systems will be invisible yet impactful, empowering users without labeling or profiling them.
- As the workplace evolves, accessibility must evolve with it—and AI is the bridge.

Chapter 17: Building an Inclusive AI Ecosystem – Community, Industry, and Academia

17.1 Introduction

An accessible future powered by AI cannot be engineered in isolation. It requires a collaborative ecosystem where academia researches inclusivity, industry innovates responsibly, and communities co-create technologies that reflect real-world needs.

This chapter explores how these three pillars—community, industry, and academia—must work in tandem to foster a culture of accessibility-first AI. We examine frameworks for collaboration, successful global models, and how India can lead the way by integrating accessibility into its digital innovation engine.

17.2 The Role of Communities in Shaping Accessible AI

1. Co-Creation, Not Just Consultation

Most AI products designed *for* people with disabilities fail when they are not designed *with* them. Community involvement must move beyond surveys or feedback loops into true co-design partnerships.

Examples:

- Inclusive hackathons where people with disabilities are co-developers.

- Design councils involving community organizations, accessibility experts, and grassroots disability rights groups.

2. Community-Driven Dataset Curation

- Communities should help define what data matters, especially for AI models used in accessibility.
- For example, Indian Sign Language datasets should be collected with ethical consent, representative diversity (region, age, dialect), and contextual usage.

3. Open Source, Grassroots Innovation

- Examples like Be My Eyes and NVDA screen reader show how open-source communities can drive large-scale accessibility.
- Community-created AI tools often address hyperlocal needs ignored by big tech.

17.3 Academia as the R&D Backbone of Inclusive AI

1. Research on Inclusive Design and Human-AI Interaction

- Universities and research labs must prioritize interdisciplinary work—AI + HCI + Disability Studies.
- Research agendas must include:
    - Explainability for disabled users
    - Ethical dataset labeling for inclusive AI

- Cross-modal learning for assistive devices

2. **Training the Next Generation**

- Curricula must include accessibility and AI ethics as core modules.
- Capstone projects, PhD theses, and AI fellowships should reward research with social impact in accessibility.

3. **Academic-Community Collaborations**

- Labs can partner with NGOs and schools for disabled children to conduct usability testing, ethnographic research, and AI prototype trials.
- Example: IIIT-Hyderabad's collaboration with SignAble Communications to develop ISL recognition models.

17.4 Industry's Role in Scaling and Sustaining Accessible AI

1. **Accessibility-by-Design Product Lifecycle**

- Companies must embed accessibility checkpoints from requirement gathering to post-launch analytics.
- Accessibility should be part of the definition of done in every agile sprint.

2. **Responsible AI Infrastructure**

- Industries should invest in:
  - Bias auditing tools
  - Accessible UX testing platforms

- Edge computing to bring AI accessibility to low-resource devices

3. Corporate Social Responsibility (CSR) and Inclusion

- CSR budgets should fund open datasets, community training programs, and grassroots accessibility innovation.
- Indian IT giants like Infosys and TCS have accessibility verticals, but startups should also lead.

4. Industry-Academia Bridge Models

- Create joint centers of excellence for AI and accessibility.
- Sponsor PhD programs, internships, and fellowships in inclusive AI.
- Host AI+Accessibility Grand Challenges with real-world use cases.

17.5 Global Models of Inclusive Ecosystems

1. Microsoft's AI for Accessibility Program

- $25 million investment in startups, researchers, and nonprofits.
- Funded tools like Seeing AI, Project Tokyo, and ASL translation systems.
- Offers APIs, mentorship, and datasets focused on disability inclusion.

2. Canada's Accessible Technology Program

- Funds accessible AI startups and community orgs building tech for seniors and people with disabilities.
- Requires community co-leadership for eligibility.

3. MIT Media Lab + Berklee Institute for Accessible Arts

- Collaborative models for inclusive music tech.
- Combines AI, arts, and disability rights.

17.6 Case Study: IIT Delhi's Center for Accessibility in AI

Overview: Established in 2024, this center brings together computer scientists, special educators, linguists, and accessibility advocates.

Initiatives:

- Multilingual ISL dataset for North Indian dialects.
- AI-powered screen reader adapted to Indian regional languages.
- Accessibility testing platform using real-world audio-visual conditions.

Impact:

- 100+ students trained in inclusive AI development.
- Partnerships with NGOs for deployment in rural schools for the deaf.

17.7 Building a Sustainable and Inclusive AI Ecosystem in India

India, with its diversity and scale, has a unique opportunity to lead globally in AI accessibility:

1. National-Level Strategy

- A dedicated National Mission on AI for Accessibility with funding, benchmarks, and policy frameworks.
- AI Accessibility Scorecard as part of DPI (Digital Public Infrastructure) assessment.

2. Grassroots and NGO Integration

- Leverage local knowledge from thousands of NGOs working with PwDs.
- Fund open translation of AI tools into Indian Sign Language and regional languages.

3. Incentivize Startups

- Offer tax breaks, AWS credits, and mentorship for startups building inclusive AI.
- Integrate accessibility testing into government procurement pipelines.

4. Community-Led Evaluation

- Establish AI Accessibility Advisory Boards composed of disability rights groups, social workers, and tech reviewers.
- Conduct regular public audits of AI accessibility in banks, transport, education, and health.

17.8 Conclusion: The Accessibility Ecosystem is the Future of AI

Accessible AI is not just a niche vertical—it's a foundational pillar for ethical, inclusive, and sustainable innovation. To truly build a society where no one is left behind, accessibility must move from the margins to the center of the AI conversation.

By uniting the wisdom of communities, the rigor of academia, and the scale of industry, we can co-create a future where AI does not merely serve a few—but empowers everyone.

Chapter 18: Roadmap and Strategy for Scaling AI Accessibility in India

18.1 Introduction

India stands at the intersection of rapid digital transformation and profound social complexity. With over 2.68 crore persons with disabilities (Census 2011), the need to design for inclusion is urgent. AI can act as a catalyst—but only when backed by a comprehensive, well-funded, and ethically grounded strategy.

This chapter outlines a concrete roadmap for scaling accessible AI solutions across India. We propose national-level interventions, ecosystem-level reforms, and specific short- and long-term strategies designed to create an inclusive digital India for all.

18.2 Strategic Vision: India's Unique Opportunity

India's diversity in languages, socio-economic contexts, and disabilities makes it a testbed for globally scalable inclusive AI. A successful model here can inform the world.

Key strengths:

- Robust public digital infrastructure (Aadhaar, UPI, DigiLocker)
- Rising AI talent pool (second-largest AI workforce globally)
- Government-led missions (Digital India, National AI Portal)

- Vibrant startup ecosystem

However, accessibility has remained a footnote in mainstream tech strategy. To scale, we must embed accessibility at the core of policy, platforms, and people.

18.3 A Four-Pillar Strategy

We propose a framework built on four foundational pillars:

1. Policy and Governance

- AI Accessibility Act: A legislative mandate ensuring AI systems procured or deployed by public bodies adhere to accessibility standards (like WCAG 2.2, BIS guidelines, etc.).
- National Accessibility Registry: Publicly available database of accessibility-compliant AI tools across education, health, transport, and e-governance.
- Inclusive Procurement Mandates: Public tenders should score vendors based on accessibility features and inclusive design practices.

2. Infrastructure and Platforms

- AI Accessibility APIs: Government-backed APIs (for ISL recognition, speech-to-text in regional languages, OCR for vernacular scripts) available via Bhashini or IndiaStack.
- Accessible Public AI Platforms: Integration of accessibility features into platforms like DigiLocker, UMANG, and eSanjeevani.

- Accessibility Cloud: Centralized compute + storage + annotation tools for NGOs/startups building assistive tech.

3. Ecosystem Enablement

- AI Accessibility Innovation Fund: ₹500 crore seed fund to support startups, NGOs, and researchers focused on inclusive AI.
- Regional Centers of Excellence (CoEs): Pan-India network of CoEs linked to academic institutions and accessibility orgs (e.g., IITs, NITs, NISH, Ali Yavar Jung Institute).
- Skill Development: Integrate AI accessibility into Skill India mission, with special focus on training PwDs in AI tool usage and data annotation.

4. Community Participation and Co-creation

- Co-Design Mandates: All government AI tools must demonstrate stakeholder engagement from disability communities.
- Community Dataset Hubs: Local communities manage data collection for underrepresented dialects, gestures, and mobility contexts.
- Open Design Repositories: Share blueprints, UX templates, and codebases for accessible AI solutions (e.g., AI screen readers, gesture input systems).

18.4 Short-Term Goals (2025–2027)

- 🚀 Launch National AI Accessibility Mission under Ministry of Electronics & IT (MeitY)

- 📊 Conduct accessibility audits of all government digital services using AI-based testers
- 🗣 Release Indian Sign Language (ISL) benchmark dataset (100+ signs) via open government platforms
- 🧠 Create NPTEL/MOOC courses on "AI for Accessibility" for upskilling developers
- 📱 Pilot AI-based ISL interpreters in government offices, police stations, and courts
- 🤝 **Mandate all Smart City programs to integrate AI-driven accessibility in transport and public infrastructure**

18.5 Long-Term Vision (2027–2030)

- 🌍 Make India a global exporter of inclusive AI tools and policies
- 📡 Enable Edge-AI Accessibility Devices (offline smart glasses, on-device OCR) at scale in rural India
- 🏫 Ensure AI tools are present in 100% of special and inclusive schools, public hospitals, and public libraries
- 🏭 Encourage Accessible AI Labs within corporates as part of ESG mandates
- 🧑‍💻 Establish "AI + Accessibility Fellowship" for innovators, educators, and community technologists

18.6 Monitoring and Evaluation

To ensure effectiveness, India needs a national monitoring framework:

Metric	Target by 2030
No. of accessible AI products	1,000+ open-source/public solutions
PwDs trained in AI usage	5 lakh individuals
Accessibility audits passed	90% of all public AI systems
Startups funded	500+ under the Innovation Fund
ISL Coverage	95% of daily-use phrases & commands

18.7 Risks, Gaps, and Mitigation

Risk/Gaps	Mitigation Strategy
Lack of diverse datasets	Fund hyperlocal data collection with communities
Tech elitism (urban bias)	Prioritize accessibility-first rural pilots
Over-centralization of strategy	Empower state-level accessibility missions
Low adoption of open standards	Offer procurement incentives for compliance

Underrepresentation of intersectional disabilities	Create targeted programs for women, tribal, and elderly PwDs

18.8 Conclusion: Toward an Accessible Tech Nation

India's AI strategy must be measured not only in economic growth, but in digital dignity. True Atma Nirbharta (self-reliance) in technology means no citizen is digitally excluded, regardless of ability.

By embracing inclusive design, investing in grassroots innovation, and fostering interdisciplinary collaboration, India can become a global beacon for ethical, scalable, and accessible AI.

Chapter 19: Impact Measurement & Accessibility KPIs

19.1 Introduction

As inclusive AI technologies proliferate, the need to measure their real-world impact becomes crucial. Without clear metrics and well-defined indicators, organizations risk falling into the trap of "checkbox accessibility" – where systems are labeled inclusive without meaningful user benefit. This chapter explores how to measure the effectiveness, reach, and equity of AI-driven accessibility initiatives through robust Key Performance Indicators (KPIs) and impact frameworks.

19.2 Why Impact Measurement Matters in Accessibility

1. Avoiding Performative Inclusion

Organizations often deploy accessible technologies to signal compliance or corporate responsibility. However, without measuring real-world change, these efforts can become hollow.

2. Driving Continuous Improvement

Well-designed KPIs enable iterative refinement by highlighting what works and what doesn't.

3. Securing Funding and Policy Support

Clear impact evidence supports proposals for grants, CSR funding, and government backing.

4. Empowering Users

Transparency about performance metrics builds trust among users with disabilities.

19.3 Defining Meaningful Accessibility KPIs

Unlike general product KPIs (e.g., engagement, churn), accessibility KPIs must account for usability, equity, and empowerment of users with disabilities. Examples include:

Category	Accessibility KPI Examples
Usability	% of users with disabilities who can complete key tasks without help
Reach	Number of unique users accessing accessibility features
Engagement	Frequency of interaction with assistive tools (e.g., screen reader toggles)
Equity	Usage across diverse disability types, geographies, and languages
Uptime & Stability	Error rates or crash frequency during assistive tool usage
Satisfaction	CSAT or NPS scores among users with disabilities
Speed of Access	Time-to-access for key functions using assistive tech
Community Co-creation	% of features developed via direct user participation

Note: KPIs must be intersectional—capturing data across disability, language, gender, and socio-economic status.

19.4 Quantitative vs Qualitative Evaluation

Both approaches are necessary for holistic measurement:

- Quantitative Data: Useful for scale and trends.
  - Surveys, usage logs, feature analytics.
  - Example: Number of voice command errors per 100 uses.
- Qualitative Data: Reveals depth and nuance.
  - Interviews, focus groups, observational studies.
  - Example: Perceived ease-of-use of gesture-based controls by deaf users.

Combining both offers a mixed-methods impact analysis.

19.5 Impact Evaluation Frameworks

Several established frameworks can be adapted for accessibility-focused AI systems:

1. Theory of Change (ToC)
   - Start with desired long-term impacts and map backward to define preconditions, activities, and outputs.
   - Encourages alignment between development efforts and social goals.
2. RE-AIM Framework (Reach, Effectiveness, Adoption, Implementation, Maintenance)

    - Originally designed for public health, this model supports evaluating broad adoption and long-term sustainability of inclusive tech.
3. Social Return on Investment (SROI)
    - Assigns monetary value to social outcomes (e.g., job opportunities created through inclusive hiring AI tools).

19.6 Community-Centered Evaluation

Evaluation is most effective when it is co-owned by users with disabilities. This can be done by:

- Partnering with disability advocacy groups to co-design surveys and KPIs.
- Incorporating Participatory Action Research (PAR) approaches.
- Creating public dashboards to share progress and accountability transparently.

19.7 Case Example: Measuring Impact in an AI Captioning System

Scenario: An AI startup implements real-time multilingual captioning in classrooms for deaf students.

Metric	Measured Outcome
Task Completion Rate	93% of students completed classwork independently
Engagement Time	Caption toggle used on average 6.2 times per session

Comprehension Scores	Improved average grades by 15% post-deployment
User Feedback (Qual.)	"I feel I finally understand the jokes and side-talk in class."
Maintenance	System downtime was under 0.5% monthly

This data was shared with school administrators and used to justify full deployment across a district.

19.8 Challenges in Accessibility Measurement

- Lack of Disaggregated Data: Disability-specific data is often unavailable.
- Over-Indexing on Usage Metrics: Tools might be used often but still fail to empower users.
- Privacy Trade-Offs: Data collection for KPIs must not compromise user dignity or anonymity.
- Context Dependency: What's effective in urban India may not apply in tribal communities.

19.9 Toward Standardized Accessibility Benchmarks

- Adoption of global standards like WCAG usage analytics or ISO 30071-1 (Digital Accessibility Maturity Model) can help normalize reporting.
- India-specific frameworks are emerging, often aligned with Accessible India Campaign (Sugamya Bharat Abhiyan) indicators.

19.10 Conclusion

Measuring the true impact of AI accessibility tools requires more than checking boxes or reporting user counts. It demands intentional, user-led KPIs that capture both breadth and depth. When done right, impact measurement is not just a feedback tool—it's a compass pointing toward a more inclusive digital future

Chapter 20: Final Reflections and Call to Action

20.1 A Journey Through Inclusion and Innovation

Over the past twenty-two chapters, we've explored the evolving relationship between Artificial Intelligence and Accessibility—not merely as separate domains, but as mutually transformative forces. We've studied algorithms, ethical frameworks, policy gaps, inclusive design methodologies, lived experiences, and revolutionary use cases. But beyond the models and metrics, one truth has emerged consistently:

Inclusion is not a feature—it's a foundation.

We are witnessing a technological renaissance, but the question remains: *Whose future is being imagined? And who gets to participate in shaping it?*

20.2 Reframing Accessibility as Innovation

For too long, accessibility has been framed as a compliance issue—something to "fix" after a product is released or as a checklist to appease legal mandates. This book has argued for a paradigm shift:

- Accessibility is innovation.
- Disabled users are not edge cases—they are drivers of design excellence.
- Assistive technologies don't just help people adapt to systems—they help systems adapt to people.

AI, with its dynamic learning and multimodal capabilities, offers a rare opportunity to rebuild digital infrastructure with *everyone* in mind.

20.3 The Moral and Market Imperative

Inclusion is not just an ethical ideal; it is a market reality:

- 15% of the world's population lives with some form of disability—representing over 1.3 billion people.
- Digital exclusion leads to lost revenue, poor user retention, and reputational harm.
- Inclusive products often serve a wider user base than originally intended—consider voice assistants, which began as assistive tech.

Governments, investors, and companies that fail to account for accessibility are not just being unjust—they're being shortsighted.

20.4 Reflections for Stakeholders

For Developers and Designers

- Bake accessibility into your code, your wireframes, and your user testing.
- Collaborate with disabled users as co-designers, not just testers.

For Policymakers

- Go beyond legislation—fund research, subsidize assistive AI, and support startups led by persons with disabilities.

For Educators and Researchers

- Make AI curriculum accessible and build inclusive research labs.
- Publish in open-access formats to ensure knowledge equity.

For Companies and Startups

- Hire inclusively, audit your AI systems for bias, and make accessibility part of your mission—not your marketing.

For Accessibility Advocates

- Keep pushing. Your voice is powerful, and your expertise is essential in shaping ethical, equitable AI futures.

20.5 Call to Action: From Awareness to Accountability

We now know what's possible. The time for *awareness* has passed—it is now a time for accountability. Let us:

- Build AI systems that do not just predict preferences, but understand limitations.
- Train models not just on data, but on empathy and equity.
- Shift from designing for the "average" user to designing for the real world's beautiful variability.

This is not only a technological revolution—it is a cultural one.

20.6 The Road Ahead

The work does not end here. In fact, it starts now:

- Contribute to open-source accessible AI.
- Mentor someone from a marginalized group entering the field.
- Start or support an accessibility initiative in your organization.
- Write, speak, advocate—become a voice for inclusive innovation.

> "We are all temporarily abled. The accessible future we build today is the world we will all need tomorrow."

Let us co-create that future—thoughtfully, equitably, inclusively.

Closing Note

As we close this book, let us remember: AI is not neutral, and technology is not inevitable. The systems we create reflect the values, biases, and aspirations of those who build them. By centering accessibility from the very beginning, we can ensure that the future we engineer is not only intelligent but equitable, empathetic, and empowering.

This book is not the conclusion of a conversation—it is a catalyst. A catalyst for developers, designers, policy makers, educators, and activists to step forward and co-create a world where inclusion is not a retrofit, but a requirement.

Let the vision of accessible, human-centered AI not remain a dream, but become our collective reality.

About DB Foundation

DB Foundation – short for **Deepali Bhavale Foundation** – is a purpose-driven non-profit organization devoted to creating a more inclusive and accessible world for individuals with disabilities. Founded with a deep personal commitment to equity and empowerment, DB Foundation stands at the intersection of compassion and innovation.

Our mission is to uplift those who are often left unheard or unseen – especially children and young adults with hearing and speech disabilities – by providing them with quality education, life skills, and the tools they need to lead independent, fulfilling lives.

Rooted in grassroots action and inspired by a bold vision for social change, DB Foundation is committed to building communities where every individual, regardless of ability, is treated with dignity, respect, and opportunity.

DB Foundation: Empowering Abilities, Redefining Futures

Our Vision

To build an inclusive India where every person with a disability has access to education, empowerment, and opportunity – not just to survive, but to thrive with pride and purpose.

We envision a future where accessibility is not an afterthought, but a foundation – woven into schools, systems, and society at large.

Our Mission

At DB Foundation, we strive to:

- Educate with dignity: Offer inclusive, accessible, and high-quality education tailored to the needs of deaf and non-verbal children.
- Empower through skills: Provide vocational training, digital literacy, and life skills that enable self-reliance and confidence.
- Innovate for inclusion: Leverage AI, assistive technology, and modern tools to bridge communication gaps and enhance access.
- Advocate for rights: Raise awareness, influence policy, and drive systemic change to promote equity and inclusion for people with disabilities.
- Collaborate for impact: Partner with educators, NGOs, corporates, and changemakers to create a sustainable ecosystem of support and inclusion.